and Bill Oatey

d in 2008 by
, 2 Clarence Place, Penzance, Cornwall TR18 2QA, UK
odge.co.uk   info@alison-hodge.co.uk

Chapman, 2008
s: David Chapman, 2008

906720-57-8

Cataloguing-in-Publication Data
cord for this book is available from the British Library.

y Christopher Laughton

riginated by BDP
ment and Production, Penzance, Cornwall

na.

Iconic Co

Sara

Davi

First publis
Alison Hod,
www.alison

© Text: Sara
© Photograp

The right of
of this work
the Copyrig

The right of
of this work
the Copyrig

ISBN-13 978-

British Librar
A catalogue r

Cover design

Designed and
Book Develop

Printed in Ch

Alison

Contents

Introduction

St Mary's, Isles of Scilly.

So many of us love Cornwall and the Isles of Scilly, with their unique culture, heritage, beauty and atmosphere. Their character is defined by the places, people, natural features and buildings that typify and represent the best of our county and the islands. In this book we aim to investigate some of those iconic locations that exemplify Cornwall – the places that fascinate, intrigue and inspire us. These are the places that we mentally picture when we think of this county; they span thousands of years, from Neolithic times to the twenty-first century.

Within Britain Cornwall and the Scillies are remote. Cornwall is a relatively thin peninsula of land stretching out into the Atlantic Ocean, almost cut off from Devon by the River Tamar. We have the longest and, many would say, the most beautiful stretch of coastline; the most westerly and the most southerly points, and some of the oldest rocks in the country which create an often rugged and impressive landscape. Cornwall's remoteness may account for the wealth of ancient monuments that remain here; perhaps people in Cornwall were able to maintain their connection with the land, and understood the importance of protecting such valuable sites as the stone circles, cromlechs (or quoits), and both hill- and cliff-top forts which can all be found here.

Unsurprisingly this landscape and its people have created and nurtured myths and legends galore. Arthurian tales crop up regularly throughout the county; tales of giants, smugglers and saints abound, and it is fascinating to reflect on these stories and how they relate to the landscape. These tales, together with the stunning landscape, have encouraged writers and artists to work in Cornwall and contribute to our heritage. Today the inspiration continues; we need look no further than The Eden Project for evidence of this.

Of course human impact has an enormous effect, from the battles and wars that led to the building of castles and defences which are scattered around the county, through to the Industrial Revolution which had a huge impact here, with large-scale mining operations, some of which continue today, and a wide array of related industries. The landscape was transformed not just by the direct effects of mining, but also by the impact of the wealth that it brought, enabling estates to be acquired and extended, gardens to blossom, and transport links to be improved.

All of the icons we have chosen for this book are based around places, so although there are many other iconic aspects to life in the county – such as the Cornish pasty

– they will have to wait for another book. Some of the locations we have chosen have been made iconic by the residents who have lived there, or by events that happen there, including Daphne du Maurier at Fowey, the choughs at Lizard Point, and gig racing on the Isles of Scilly.

Perhaps we are biased, but Cornwall seems to be packed with iconic locations that enrapture, enthral and instruct us. It has been difficult to select only about 100 locations and squeeze them into 60 chapters, and maybe you would have included others; but that is part of the wonder of this place – it can mean different things to different people.

Note that our icons are arranged alphabetically in this book. There are notes regarding access for each icon on pages 126–7. General information may be obtained from Visit Cornwall (tel. 01872 322900, www.cornwalltouristboard.co.uk); English Heritage (tel. 0870 333 1181, www.english-heritage.org.uk); the Isles of Scilly Tourist Information Centre (tel. 01720 422536, www.simplyscilly.co.uk), or the National Trust (tel. 0870 458 4000, www.nationaltrust.org.uk).

Sarah Chapman
2008

Abbey Garden, Tresco

Right: Ruins of an abbey are situated in the garden.
Above: A series of cleverly situated focal points lead the eye into the garden.

You have to be a determined traveller to visit the Abbey Garden on Tresco: it isn't the sort of place you could just drop into on your way past. Visitors either come direct to Tresco via the helicopter service, or by boat from one of the other Islands. For this much effort you expect something special, and Tresco has special by the bucketful!

The island itself is a haven of peace and tranquillity; the white sandy beaches stretching around the southern sections are a coast lover's dream, and these contrast markedly with a rocky and impressive northern section of the island. Tresco is the only island in this archipelago in private ownership; the others are part of the Duchy of Cornwall. The Dorrien-Smith family, who own the island, have maintained the mystical, while caring for and enhancing a thriving island and garden.

Augustus Smith bought the island in the 1830s, and as an enthusiastic plant collector immediately saw the potential of this climatic haven, where winter doesn't really exist. He established a sub-tropical garden with plants from around the globe, based around the remains of a twelfth-century priory. Many of the plants are simply too tender to grow anywhere on mainland Britain. Tresco is one of the few places on the Isles of Scilly where a significant number of trees can be found; here a wealth of evergreens have been used to form shelter from the strong, salt-laden winds that rush across the islands.

Covering just under 7 hectares this may be a relatively small garden, but a series of terraced paths and steep slopes generate a number of long, directed views as well as intimate cameos. The views are often enhanced by glimpses of neighbouring islands but, as if this were not enough, sculptures have been cleverly placed to add further attractions. One of these, standing at the foot of the long, straight Lighthouse Walk, is of the three eldest children of Robert Dorrien-Smith, the present owner of Tresco. It seems appropriate that the statue of Gaia (the Earth-mother from Greek Mythology) has been situated in a more secluded position nearby. One of my favourites, because of all the bird activity it generates, is the water feature in the shape of an agave near the entrance to the gardens, which acts as one of a series of focal points visible from the entrance.

Also within the garden there is a museum of ship's figureheads, called the Valhalla. This fascinating collection is a poignant reminder of the huge number of ships that have foundered on the treacherous rocks around these islands.

With plants from around 80 countries situated in one of the most beautiful spots in the county, the Abbey Garden will appeal to anyone with even the vaguest interest in gardens.

Cornwall has more coastline than any other county in England. With 697 kilometres of it reaching out into the Atlantic Ocean there are many iconic locations along its length – none more so than the famous Bedruthan Steps.

Bedruthan Steps, to the north of Newquay, is one of our more dramatic and dynamic stretches of coastline; its ever-changing forms have captured imaginations for many years. Victorian tourists began to visit this area to see the coastline and the location of famous wrecks like the *Samaritan*, which sank in 1846 after colliding with one of the stacks now named in its memory. It epitomizes the eroded, gnarled, rock-strewn cliff that accounts for much of our coast; and like so many of Cornwall's coastal gems this rocky environment contrasts well with the stunning sandy coves exposed at low tide.

Left: The sea stacks of Bedruthan Steps.
Above: Thrift grows on the cliffs near Bedruthan Steps.

The Devonian rock here is in fact quite resistant to the pounding waves. It may not immediately appear so, but the fact that the cliffs, rock stacks and pillars reach up to around 70 metres is testament to their hardness. It is the network of small cracks and weaknesses that allows the sea to penetrate and lead to such spectacular erosion. The cliffs here are subjected to occasional rock falls and landslips. The National Trust, which owns the area, closes off the main steps to the beach in winter when there is a greater danger of sudden falls.

The beach is certainly worth a visit at low tide; the twists and cuts in the rocks are spectacular. Creep around the edges of caves; circle the sea stacks where the more resilient sections of rock still resist wave beating, or just enjoy the sandy stretches. The fact that this geological paradise is only available at limited times between high tides makes it even more exciting. But beware the ocean here: the currents, as on many parts of our coast, make swimming dangerous; at the cliff top a plaque to the memory of Alex Laurie who drowned here in 1903 exemplifies this. Waves powerful enough to carve such a coastline should not be trusted.

The views along this stretch of coast are wonderful at any time. If you want to see Cornwall's coast at its dramatic best, then Bedruthan Steps will not disappoint.

Boscastle Harbour

The north coast of Cornwall is rugged and wild. When lashed by heavy seas there are few places of safety for mariners caught out here. Boscastle harbour is an exception, for the twisting shape of its valley as it enters the sea has created one of Cornwall's most awe-inspiring natural harbours.

Standing on the headland of Willapark during a storm, it is clear that even the mighty forces of the Atlantic are calmed before the waves reach the inner harbour, where boats have moored since Elizabethan times. The harbour itself was built in 1584 by Sir Richard Grenville, and is little changed since that time. Boscastle was once an important port, trading with South Wales, Bristol, and ports along the English south coast.

This stretch of coast cannot fail to capture the imagination; after all, some of the most famous literary figures have been inspired by Boscastle. In his epic Arthurian poem, Lord Tennyson wrote of King Arthur departing for Lyonesse from Boscastle harbour. The author and poet Thomas Hardy met his first wife, Emma, while working at St Juliot's church just outside the town. The church now has a memorial window dedicated to the poet. Perhaps more importantly, the cliffs around Boscastle feature in Hardy's poems, and in his novel *A Pair of Blue Eyes*. These cliffs are the highest in Cornwall, reaching 223 metres. Particularly memorable is Beeny Cliff, where Hardy describes Emma riding her horse along the cliff line – young, beautiful and at one with her surroundings.

Today, much of the land around Boscastle is owned by the National Trust, including, to the south, inland of Willapark, the Forrabury Stitches. The 'stitches' are strips of land which pre-date enclosure, and are managed using the same methods as were used in the medieval period. Many rare types of flowers which grow among our crops, known as arable weeds, have survived here and can be found particularly around the edges of the 'strips' in the summer. The cliffs and offshore islands around Boscastle are a haven for seabirds, including razorbills and guillemots.

It is an irony that on a coast where the sea can prove so dangerous, the biggest threat to Boscastle in recent years came from inland. The flash flood of August 2004 caused the River Valency to wreak havoc in the centre of Boscastle, but the people refused to let it destroy the character of their village. Boscastle is everything it ever has been, and more.

Right: Boscastle Harbour.
Above: This window, in St Juliot's Church,
is dedicated to Thomas Hardy.

Cornish tin miners are world-famous for their ability to extract ore in unlikely situations, and there aren't many situations less likely than the shafts that stretch out under the sea from the Botallack mine, near St Just in Penwith.

The mineral lodes in this area lie perpendicular to the coastline, and therefore stretch out to sea; they are narrow and dip almost vertically, so shafts have to be deep and extensive to reach the precious ores. Evidence suggests that mining has taken place here for thousands of years, with the easier lodes being worked from the surface as early as the Iron Age. As time went by miners went ever further underground, and progressively further from land, so that by 1778 William Pryce noted that the mine here was being worked 80 fathoms, or 146 metres, out to sea. (Cornish mine distances were measured in fathoms. A fathom is 1.83 metres, or the distance between the fingertips with both arms outstretched.)

What also marks Botallack as different from other mines is the precarious cliff-top position of its engine houses, known as The Crowns. It was necessary to build these houses here because at that time shafts had to be dug by hand-drilling, and it would have taken well over a year to get the shaft close to sea level from the top of the cliff. The first engine was probably in place here at the beginning of the nineteenth century but, at that time, the mine was not profitable, and it was thought to be exhausted soon after. It was sold to Stephen Harvey James in 1836, and, as it turned out, he made a shrewd investment. It took a few years to pay off, but by the 1840s tin and copper were being produced in unprecedented quantities, and shareholders reaped high dividends. Shafts expanded, eventually reaching 250 fathoms down and over half a mile out to sea. This level of extraction required new and better winding engines, and The Crowns engine houses were rebuilt. The lower of the two was erected in 1835, and the other in 1862. The latter pulled a specially built 'gig' or box along a diagonal shaft stretching out to sea. As with many Cornish mines this one had its disasters: in 1863 the chain pulling the gig snapped, leaving eight men and a boy to hurtle to their deaths.

As the nineteenth century ended, the price of tin fell and that, combined with flooding problems, led to the closure of Botallack mine. There were several attempts to reopen the mine, most recently in the 1980s, but a fall in the price of tin in 1985 put an end to that. Sadly the age of the Cornish tin mine was ending; today we are left to marvel at the prowess of the engineers, and wonder at the bravery of the miners, who made profit from Botallack mine.

Left: The Crowns engine houses at Botallack.
Above: Thrift grows on the cliffs at Botallack.

Caerhays has a wondrous setting: a fairytale castle in a wooded valley adjacent to a large, sweeping lake and a quiet, sandy beach. Each of these features enhances the estate and its reputation, but it is most well known for the surrounding gardens, which in spring are truly beautiful.

The gardens of Caerhays are important because they hold a National Magnolia Collection. These trees flower profusely in spring, and it is at this time that the garden is open for all to enjoy it. Holding a National Collection means having at least 75 per cent of all species listed for that particular plant; these must be clearly labeled and displayed for the public to view. In addition, the collection holder must aim to increase the collection by adding any other types of the particular plant. As part of their work, the gardeners here are constantly looking for new cultivars, raising and adding these to the collection of magnolias. In the collection at Caerhays there are over 40 named species, and there are many more cultivars to be added to the collection in years to come.

Left: Caerhays Castle in early spring.
Above: A magnolia flower at Caerhays.

Gardening may be the most significant aspect of Caerhays today, but this has not always been the case. The estate has a long history. It belonged to the Trevanion family from 1370 to 1840, and it was in the early nineteenth century that John Bettesworth Trevanion thought of bettering the home he had inherited, and employed the architect John Nash to redesign the house. Nash created an imposing castle, but at great expense – sadly too much for Trevanion, who fell heavily into debt and was eventually forced to flee to Paris, leaving Caerhays to fall into disrepair. The house remained empty until 1853 when it was bought by the successful local businessman Michael Williams, who began the transformation we see today. The estate is still owned by the Williams family; neither Michael nor his son spent much of their time here, but Michael's grandson, John Charles Williams (JCW), inherited the house in 1880 and began to transform the estate. Here was a man with a passion for plants and a particular interest in hybridization. He worked with camellias, daffodils and rhododendrons as well as magnolias. Many of the plants were grown from seeds brought directly from China, collected by those sent out to search for new varieties and plants by the leading garden specialists of the day. Many of these early garden additions can still be seen today. JCW transformed this estate, and created a garden that is a delight for both the casual visitor and the plant enthusiast. In spring Caerhays Castle is truly a memorable location.

Carn Brea

Right: The Carn Brea monument.
Above: Carn Brea Castle at sunrise.

Carn Brea is undoubtedly a major Cornish landmark: the hill can be seen from all around the west of the county, and the shape of the monument and castle are easy to recognize, even in silhouette against the skyline.

The granite hill on which these icons stand is 230 metres high, and this commanding position means that it has a long history of occupation. Excavations in the 1970s unearthed a neolithic settlement on the site, probably large enough to accommodate between 100 and 200 people. These ancient people chose a site that was easy to defend, with a wide-ranging view over much of the surrounding coast and landscape. It is easy to imagine how this could be a sought-after location all those thousands of years ago, and presumably occupation was continuous from that time onwards. There is evidence that the site was adapted in the Iron Age, by creating a more organized hill fort, and building houses inside its ramparts. This ancient settlement was situated between the castle and monument which we see on the hill today, but it is mostly invisible, appearing only as odd stones. Our more recent use of this hill top is through the current castle, which was first established in the fourteenth or fifteenth century, and was built by the Bassett family originally as a hunting lodge. The building we see today has been extensively renovated and updated since that time, until its most recent reincarnation as a restaurant.

From a distance the monument on the peak of the hill looks like a cross, but when you get closer it is a huge, 27-metres high hexagonal obelisk. This impressive structure was erected in 1836 to the memory of Francis Bassett, Lord de Dunstaville. The Bassett family were important mine- and landowners in the area; their family seat was at Tehidy. Francis Bassett was concerned with the conditions experienced by men working underground, and did much to improve the welfare of miners working in his mines. When he died these mines closed for the day, to allow an estimated 20,000 people to form a procession at his funeral.

Carn Brea forms one of three granite peaks in this part of Cornwall; the other two are St Agnes Beacon and Carn Marth. As the highest of the three it has the most commanding views, and is a good place to look across the former mining landscape of the Camborne-Redruth area.

Carn Euny

Right: Carn Euny settlement.
Above: Carn Euny fogou.

It was during the Iron Age (approximately 700 BC to AD 43) that the Celts started to live in defended settlements with bank and ditch enclosures. One example of such a settlement is at Carn Euny in West Penwith. The wonderful thing about the ancient monuments of West Penwith is that many of them are so well preserved and so accessible. At Carn Euny visitors can walk freely around the site, and inspect the remains of round houses and their associated courtyards in quite an extensive and complex arrangement. Archaeological evidence from the site shows that the first habitation here was built between 500 and 300 BC. Initially the houses would have been of timber construction, but these were replaced by stone houses from around 50 BC. At some point between the second and fourth centuries AD these houses were replaced, or reworked into courtyard houses. The outlines of the houses are well preserved, and in some cases reveal interior details such as fireplaces and recesses in walls. Occupation at Carn Euny ended around AD 400 when the site was abandoned.

Even without any further intrigue the Carn Euny site would have been worthy of inclusion in this book, but within its boundaries is concealed another iconic Cornish feature – the fogou. Fogous are found only in Cornwall; their name derives from the Cornish word for a cave, which reflects a little of their design. They consist of an underground passage, sometimes with connecting chambers. Their purpose remains a mystery, but theories include their being special places of worship or ritual; places to hide from attack, or simply somewhere to store food – a sort of early larder.

All known fogous are associated with settlements, and their creation would have taken considerable effort, so they obviously had some function for these communities. The fogou at Carn Euny dates from the early part of the Iron Age; here it is thought that the large, stone-lined chamber, which is circular and 5 metres in diameter, was constructed first. The adjoining passage, which is just over 10 metres long, was added later. Access to the passage would once have been through a small hole; the larger access point now available was added at a much later date.

Fogous are found mostly in Penwith, but one of the longest examples is Halliggye fogou near Trelowarren; this has a passageway of about 30 metres in length. At other sites, such as Chysauster (in Penwith), only small sections remain.

Castle-an-Dinas

Cornwall has more than its fair share of Iron-Age cliff castles and hill forts, probably because the Celts had valuable resources such as tin and copper which they needed to be able to trade in safety. Although relatively well preserved for their age, many of the remains of these castles take no little imagination to interpret, but there are some which are still very impressive.

Many of the headlands in West Cornwall have evidence of cliff castles. The more remote the headland, and the narrower its neck, the more likely it is to have been used. Look for evidence in the shape of a ditch or mound across the neck of a headland. Often these cliff castles were no more than safe places at which to trade, though in some cases evidence has been found of habitation within the defensive fortifications. Good examples of cliff castles and hill forts in West Cornwall can be seen at Gurnard's Head, and nearby Bosigran Head near Pendeen; Logan Rock near Porthcurno, and Lankidden near Coverack on the Lizard.

Clues to the presence of a cliff castle include not only the geographical; another tip is to look at the name of the headland. If the name contains the words *treen* (aka *treryn* or *trereen*), which means 'farm by a castle'; *caer* (aka *car*), which means an enclosure or fort, or obviously 'castle', then the likelihood is that a castle or fort was present at some point. The term 'castle' has to be interpreted in the context of the age in which it was built. These are not the huge stone castles of medieval times but a variety of walls, ditches and mounds that would once have been topped by wooded structures.

The word *dinas* means 'high place', and so Castle-an-Dinas is literally 'a castle on a high place'. There are at least two places in Cornwall named 'Castle-an-Dinas': one is near Penzance and is impressive, but probably more impressive is the one near Indian Queens. This castle is certainly on a high place, and has wonderful 360°panoramic views.

Castle-an-Dinas, Indian Queens, is one of the largest of its kind in Cornwall, and is marked by three huge, circular earth banks and ditches. It was occupied between 400 BC and AD 150: evidence of this comes in the form of post holes, sling stones and pottery. Inside the fort there are two Bronze Age burial mounds, which would have been in use more than a thousand years before the Iron Age people created their castle, but these burial sites were left intact, showing how much they were respected.

Left: Castle-an-Dinas, near Indian Queens, has three concentric ramparts. Above: Bosigran cliff castle is typical of ancient coastal fortifications.

Charlestown harbour was developed as a Georgian 'new town' between 1790 and 1810 by Charles Rashleigh, founder of the china clay industry in Cornwall. He employed John Smeaton – famous for his lighthouse construction – to oversee the building of the harbour, and in so doing transformed the tiny village of West Polmear. Understandably, the new port took the name of its founder and became 'Charlestown'. It was not just china clay that was shipped from this port; tin and copper from nearby mines were also exported. This was particularly true in the early years of the harbour's existence, during the Napoleonic wars, when these metals were in great demand. In just one period of four months in 1813, 3,792 tons of copper were shipped out on 49 separate ships. Evidence of this frantic activity is still obvious around the small but sheltered harbour: old warehouses, net houses and even tunnels are still very much in evidence.

By the middle of the nineteenth century the harbour had become an important base for the processing and exporting of pilchards, which added to its success and wealth. It is said that at the zenith of this industry, in 1847, some 122 million fish were exported from Charlestown in a year, but like tin mining, this industry started to decline before the end of that century.

With the loss of its staple industries, the port might also have declined. Thankfully this was not the case. Charlestown is remarkable in that it remains so little altered; this applies to the surrounding homes and other buildings as much as to the harbour itself. The 'olde worlde' appearance of the area is enhanced by the presence of square-rigged ships which berth here; although these appear to be museum pieces they remain seaworthy, and these beautiful, tall sailing vessels are open to the public during the summer. The ships have been used in many television programmes and films, some of the more famous of which include *Treasure Island*, *The Three Musketeers*, *Hornblower* and *Shackleton*. But it isn't just the ships that are used for these productions: the whole harbour area comes to a standstill when the film crews are 'in town'.

Details of the harbour's history can be viewed at the Charlestown Shipwreck and Heritage Centre, but the unique feature of Charlestown is the feeling of stepping back in time.

Left: Charlestown Harbour.
Above: Rigging on one of the old ships at Charlestown.

China Clay Tips

Right: A conical china clay tip.
Above: A view of the china clay country from Roche Rock.

The granite in Cornwall formed around 300 million years ago; when the molten rock bubbled up through the ground the intense heat impacted on everything around it. One of the minerals found in granite is known as feldspar, and in some areas of Cornwall, most significantly around St Austell, the feldspar readily decomposes into a fine powder. This fine-grained, soft, white powder is called kaolinite, and it is on this insignificant-looking material that a large proportion of the Cornish economy has been based for the last couple of centuries. This is the substance that we know as china clay.

China clay was first discovered by William Cookworthy on Tregonning Hill near Helston, where it was subsequently quarried to a limited extent; but it is in the hills around St Austell where the largest Cornish reserves were found. The first uses for this substance were also developed by Cookworthy, a chemist based in Plymouth, who first produced and patented a kind of porcelain using the substance. This triggered a great demand for the clay, which quickly became a major local industry employing thousands. China clay is now used in the paper industry to put a fine coating on the paper, and in paint production to create a thick, smooth paint. It is used in pharmaceuticals and cosmetics, as well as many other industries worldwide.

This would be a winning story were it not for the waste. For each tonne of china clay produced, nine tonnes of waste are created. Given that Cookworthy began his production in the late eighteenth century, that means a lot of waste: in excess of 500 million tonnes and counting. With no real means of using this waste it was left in tips with little thought given to its impact on the environment. Early workings left behind small conical tips; more recently waste was heaped into long, flat-topped mounds, which were thought to be more stable. Of course, the clay extraction leaves huge holes in the ground, so some of the waste was used to fill these as extraction progressed. Other craters were converted into lakes and reservoirs, and most recently one very large hole was filled by the Eden Project.

Waste got everywhere. The St Austell River is also known as the White River; the Fal has an amazingly large amount of silt, while around Par white silt covered the port. Compared with other forms of industrial waste this is fairly harmless, but there can be no denying that the mountains of waste have huge visual impact. On this barren, infertile medium it takes a long time for vegetation to take hold, but in our more recent environmentally aware society some assistance has been given to help soften the edges of these waste tips by sowing the seeds of wildflowers and trees. Heathland species can survive here, so heathers have been planted by collecting local seed and spreading it over vast areas of ground. A good area to see the effect of this regeneration of the environment is at Caerloggas Down.

Come-to-Good

George Fox, who founded the Religious Society of Friends, known as Quakers, first came to Cornwall in 1656, bringing with him the radical ideas of this new religious group. His opinions about concepts such as sin were at odds with the orthodoxy of the time, and were held to be blasphemous; as a result he was arrested on several occasions in Britain, including once in Cornwall. He was taken first to Bodmin, and then to Launceston jail where he was held for several weeks. He kept a detailed journal of this period and his subsequent trial. When he was not incarcerated, and despite official opposition, many followers in Cornwall came to hear him speak, and so the Quaker message, extolling an individual relationship with God, spread. A group of Quakers (or Friends) met near Truro from the 1680s, and built a simple but attractive cob and thatch meeting house at Come-to-Good in 1710.

Quaker meetings are mostly silent, without rite or ceremony, and the Friends' desire for simplicity is apparent in the simple structure of this meeting house. Here is a religious building without ostentation, reflecting the ideals of its creators. From the outside its immaculate white walls, shuttered windows and extensive thatched roof come together to produce a most appealing structure. On the inside the walls are also whitewashed, and stand without ornamentation. The pews that line the walls are focused on a central table, while at one end is a stand or gallery, used to address a meeting. Either side of this are settles, or benches, which may originally have been placed against the walls. With no adornments to distract, the eye is drawn to the beauty of the wooden wall panelling; the pillars supporting the balcony; the beams of the roof vault, and the carefully laid thatching. Even the window panes are eye catching: the glass is original, and is thought to have been recycled from another, even earlier, building.

Right: The Friends Meeting House at Come-to-Good.
Above: Inside the meeting house.

This meeting house has maintained its original features and integrity; the only significant change in structure since its formation is a twentieth-century extension to the rear. The building is kept open for everyone to enjoy and to use for worship, and is well worth a visit. It would be difficult to find a more tranquil building: here is truly a place of peace.

Cot Valley

Right: The view from Porth Nanven.
Above: The rounded stones on the beach are an attraction at Cot Valley.

There can't be many places in the world where the shape of the stones on the beach have attracted quite as much attention as they have at the mouth of the Cot Valley, near St Just in Penwith.

This small valley has long been most significant for its mining activity, with copper and tin being extracted by tin streaming as early as the Bronze Age, but in a more organized fashion from the medieval period. The river provided the power for mills, and the remains of old buildings, buddles (troughs for washing crushed ore) and other structures can still be seen. In recent times more human attention has been focused on the beach at the foot of the valley, known as Porth Nanven. There can be no doubting that this is an attractive spot with views reaching out to the Isles of Scilly past the distinctive rocky islets known as the Brisons (the profile of which some locals reckon looks like Charles de Gaulle lying in a bath!).

Rather than the view, it is the rocks on the beach that have become iconic. Technically, these rocks are boulders, because they have a diameter of more than 25 centimetres, and beaches composed of boulders are relatively uncommon. The majority of the boulders on the beach here are very smoothly worn. The story of their formation is told on an interpretive board underneath the cliff at the top of the beach, and this story can be seen within the cliff itself. Looking at the cliff you will see that the rounded boulders are found at the bottom, and packed on top are more angular rock fragments. The rounded boulders were worn by the sea rolling them around, taking off the sharp edges until they were perfectly smooth. As the sea levels dropped during the last Ice Age, these stones were left high and dry. Gradually the smooth stones were packed in with debris from the surrounding hill tops, and shards of sharper rocks slipped down the slopes on top. Then with the end of the Ice Age came a rise in sea levels, and the waves began cutting back into the cliffs. Released from their incarceration, the stones now roll around on the beach again.

Recently the stones made the news when some were stolen by people from distant parts of the country for their gardens, and others were used for displays in civic areas. It was even more newsworthy when some people were made to return them!

Photographers hold this beach in high esteem, and it is quite common to see images captured at Porth Nanven in photographic exhibitions around the world.

The Eden Project

Right: One of the Eden biomes.
Above: Inside the core building at Eden.

Opened in 2001, The Eden Project is 'a living theatre of plants and people', demonstrating our dependence on plants. It has shot to fame on a wave of publicity generated by its spectacular, often record-breaking, construction statistics.

Eden was built on wasteland in a 60-metres deep, 15-hectare china clay pit. When preparing the site, contractors had to move 1.8 million tonnes of ground in about six months. The drainage system, put in place before construction began, has to cope with vast quantities of water, including an estimated 43 million gallons in the first three months.

The scaffolding erected to build the biomes is officially the world's largest ever free-standing scaffold structure, and used 46,000 poles.

The list goes on: the humid tropics biome is 240 metres long, 110 metres wide, and 55 metres high. The warm temperate biome is 135 metres long, 65 metres wide, and 35 metres high. The biomes are made from 625 hexagonal windows; each window comprises three layers of a very lightweight clear film called ethylenetetrafluoroethylene, inflated with air into 2-metres-deep pillows. The largest window is 11 metres across.

The humid tropics biome now houses over 2,000 species of carefully selected tropical plants in an environment that allows them to reach their full potential. The air in this biome is kept at temperatures varying between 18° and 35°C.

Over a million people visit Eden each year, with a staggering 1.8 million in the first full year. It is thought that, in its first five years, Eden contributed £700 million to the local economy.

Even the plants have some impressive statistics: one of them – the tropical bamboo, *Bambusa gigantica* – can grow up to 45 centimetres a day. In spring more than 300,000 daffodil bulbs are planted.

Unlike its air-filled windows, we can be sure that Eden will never remain inert. Change is constant, from year to year and across the seasons. Of the many major developments since the erection of the domes, it is perhaps the construction of the Core that has attracted most interest. This building houses a range of exhibits which challenge the way we think about our environment. More than this Eden, through the Eden Foundation, contributes to environmental research projects such as climate and waste management, supporting development initiatives in many countries.

Return visits throughout the year, to experience the full range of plants that flourish here, are encouraged with very good price deals. As well as being of record-breaking proportions, The Eden Project is informative, innovative, ever-changing and educational, but most of all it is impressive.

Fistral Beach

Right: Fistral Beach.
Above: Surfing a wave.

Huge, powerful waves are a feature of the Cornish coast, and what could be more exciting than to be travelling landward with one? Waves: all that raw energy, spray scattering in every direction, and an amazing forward momentum. Surfing is now big business in Cornwall.

Surfing is centuries old, but first came to the attention of Westerners in reports of locals riding waves logged by Captain Cook when he visited Tahiti and Hawaii. Sadly, when the British missionaries arrived in these islands they tried to stop surfing as a frivolous and possibly suggestive activity. But people were not deterred, and a passion for surfing continued and then positively boomed in the twentieth century.

For successful surfing you need significant waves. The size of a wave is a function of the distance the wind has blown over the sea: the greater the uninterrupted distance the larger the waves are likely to be. The best surfing locations in the world – Australia, Hawaii and Newquay – all have coasts with a huge, unbroken stretch of ocean beyond. In Cornwall, winds blow across the full extent of the Atlantic from the Americas, uninterrupted by land.

There are many surfing locations around the coast of Cornwall, but it is Fistral Beach, Newquay, that is the best known and the home of the world surf championships. In surfing terms, Fistral is our equivalent of Bondi, Waikiki or Malibu; the waves here in Cornwall are powerful, and often 1.5 to 2.5 metres high. It is indeed one of the best places in the world to take to a surf board. The beach faces west-northwest, which means it picks up good swell, and has consistent sandbanks capable of holding on to this. At the north end of Fistral, Cribbar Rocks on the tip of Towan Head produce massive waves, only to be tackled by the bravest, or most foolhardy, of surfers. Apparently waves of around 6 metres have been ridden here. Unsurprisingly Newquay has developed a surf culture; here you can find surf schools, board and clothing sales, and a huge surf following.

If surfing appeals, then Cornwall is a premier location to both learn and practise this sport; and if the waves are a little flat then there are always the surrounding beaches, cliffs and scenery to occupy you.

Fowey

Some towns have all the luck! A picturesque setting, successful port, charming streets, great fishing and now a thriving festival, Fowey is truly unique. Of course, these attributes helped to establish its literary credentials; after all it was the home for many years of Sir Arthur Quiller Couch, and Fowey features as 'Troy' in many of his novels. It was also a favourite location of Kenneth Grahame, whose tales of the river bank started in the form of letters written from the town. Today Fowey remains a thriving harbour, exporting china clay all around the world, and with a yacht club, of which Quiller Couch was Commodore, still at the heart of a busy sailing community, and home to the annual regatta.

Most of all though, Fowey is inexorably linked to the life and work of Daphne du Maurier; much of her adult life was spent in and around this coastal town, and many of her famous novels were written here. Today the area hosts the du Maurier Festival, with a range of events that attract many people to this part of south Cornwall.

Left: Ferryside at Fowey is Du Maurier's one-time home.
Above: Shops in Fowey's main street.

As a child du Maurier visited Cornwall on family holidays, but she began to cement her links with Fowey when the family took Ferryside, a small cottage alongside the river, as a holiday home when Daphne was 19. It was here that she wrote her first novel, *The Loving Spirit*, and here that she met Major Frederick Browning, the man who was to become her husband. In the early years of their marriage the couple lived in London, but during the Second World War Daphne and her children came to Fowey, and in 1943 she moved to the house that she loved and with which she is most associated – Menabilly, on Gribbin Head. In 1969, four years after her husband had died, she moved to her final home at Kilmarth.

Cornwall inspired du Maurier; it provides the setting for much of her writing and the stunning backdrop for so many scenes. It is possible to trace the character of Cornwall through her writing; she understood the nature of the county, and the treachery of the weather and the sea. Good examples of this include the harsh conditions on Bodmin Moor described in *Jamaica Inn* (1936), or those that lead to locating the small boat in *Rebecca* (1938). Menabilly is probably the inspiration for Mandalay in *Rebecca*, while *Frenchman's Creek* (1941) is set around the Helford River, and in *My Cousin Rachel* (1951) Ambrose owns a large estate on the Cornish coast. In fact, throughout her writing the inspiration of the county can be seen – not just in her fiction; she also wrote about Cornwall itself, perhaps the wonderful *Vanishing Cornwall* (1967) being the best known example. There have been other Cornish authors, and other authors based in Cornwall, but none so closely linked to the county as du Maurier.

Her life and work are now celebrated by the annual du Maurier Festival based in Fowey, which is held around the time of her birthday. Each year in May artists, writers and musicians gather to celebrate and perform. There can be no doubt that du Maurier helped to put Cornwall on to the literary map, and this festival is certainly helping to raise the profile of both the county and the author.

Gig Racing

Right: A lady's gig race from Nut Rock to Hugh Town.
Above: The Garrison, St Mary's.

The gig is a traditional Cornish rowing boat with a fascinating, sometimes rather disturbing, history and an exciting present.

Gigs were used for a variety of purposes, including the rescue of sailors, salvaging of wrecks, smuggling, and the servicing of lighthouses, to name but a few. It is thought that gig racing has its origins in the eighteenth century, when the rowing boats would take a pilot out to the large sailing ships waiting a safe distance from the Cornish coast to be brought securely into harbour. The pilot to reach the sailing ship first would get the job and therefore the payment, so if more than one crew spotted a waiting ship, then the fastest gig would get the commission.

Gigs are built to a standard design, traditionally of Cornish elm. They are 32 feet long and 4 feet 3 inches wide across their beam. There are eight seats, so that six rowers and a coxswain can sit with a spare seat in the bow. The rowers sit alternately three on each side. This standard comes from *The Treffry*, built at St Mawes in 1838, which is raced by the Newquay club to this day. The gig is said to be the ideal shape to cope with Cornish waters, although the number of rowers was partly dictated by Customs and Excise, whose boats could be out-rowed by gigs with more than six rowers on board!

Gig racing has grown in popularity since the 1960s, and today there are over 50 gigs in Devon, Cornwall and the Isles of Scilly. The World Championships have been held on Scilly since 1990, and the popularity of the sport continues to grow. Gig racing is a major sport on Scilly – crews race weekly through the spring and summer months, taking on boats from as far afield as Australia in the world championships during May.

On Scilly the Islanders race each week between Nut Rock and St Mary's harbour, the women on a Wednesday and the men on a Friday. The spectacle is popular, and boats packed with locals and tourists follow the gigs during the race. The best land-based viewing point is on the Garrison, which, reaching a height of 42 metres, is one of the higher points on the islands, and certainly the highest near the harbour. It seems appropriate to watch the traditional sport of gig racing from this historic defensive headland, whose initial fortifications date back to the reign of Elizabeth I.

Godrevy

Right: A tumultuous sea at Godrevy Point.
Above: Grey seals in Mutton Cove.

In a county with a long coastline and great maritime tradition, it shouldn't come as a surprise to see a lot of lighthouses. Of them all it is the one at Godrevy which is probably most admired by visitors and locals alike. It is difficult to imagine a more impressive location than this rocky island just off shore at the mouth of St Ives Bay. Here tumultuous seas and dangerous rocks mark the boundary between the precipitous north coast and the more sheltered, sweeping sandy bay that stretches all the way to St Ives.

Today the coastline around Gwithian and Godrevy is a popular location for bucket-and-spade holidays, evening strolls, or just somewhere to watch the sun go down. A few hundred years ago the action would have been rather different, as this was a busy and dangerous shipping area. Ships and their crews were often lost around the Cornish coast, but it was the loss of one ship in particular that led to the construction of the Godrevy lighthouse in the nineteenth century. The 700-ton steamer, the *Nile*, perished on the rocks here in 1854 with all her crew and passengers.

The task of building the lighthouse began in early 1858, and the 26-metres high tower was first illuminated in March 1859. It might seem that this would be a straightforward place to build; the island is above the high-tide mark and close to shore. But at one point the workforce was marooned on Godrevy Island for a fortnight in bad weather, and on another occasion almost 1,000 people landed in good weather to see the work in progress, and inevitably were rather in the way of any progress.

The National Trust acquired the site around Godrevy Head in the 1930s; at that time it was common for visitors to be rowed out to the light to visit the lighthouse keepers in summer. Perhaps this is how Virginia Woolf got the idea of a family trip rowing to a lighthouse in *To The Lighthouse* (1927), as she spent holidays in the area. Until 1934 the lighthouse was manned, but since that time it has been automatic, converting to solar power in 1995.

The headland of Godrevy is also interesting for its wildlife: in particular there is a regular group of grey seals which bask on the beach in Mutton Cove, just to the east of the point. In summer you won't find a busier National Trust car-park in Cornwall than the one at Godrevy, but the best times to visit are when a wind is blowing and everyone else stays home!

Goonhilly Earth Station

Right: The huge dish known as Arthur, seen at sunset.
Above: A close-up of Arthur.

We take for granted the fact that any major event, anywhere in the world – a new president, a world cup, a major concert – can be viewed live. Someone can be half way around the world and yet appear in front of you on a television screen. This is a recent phenomenon made possible by a very special Cornish location – Goonhilly Earth Station. Many aspects of the communications industry, including telephone calls, fax data, computer links and television, all pass through Goonhilly.

This all started in 1962 when the first dish or antenna, named Arthur, was built to track the Telstar satellite, and for the first time pictures from America were transmitted into British homes. In the early hours of a July morning, the rather blurred picture of the chairman of the American Telephone & Telegraph Company (AT&T) appeared on television screens as the first signals were captured by this huge dish. Arthur set the standard and soon other dishes, both here and around the world, were tracking and relaying signals.

Dishes varied in size and, as technology moved forwards, composition. There were over 60 dishes on site at Goonhilly, huge antennae pointing skywards; many were named after characters in the Arthurian stories, Merlin being the largest built here with a diameter of 32 metres, and Arthur the heaviest, weighing 1,118 tonnes, yet with the capability to turn through 360° in less than three minutes. The history of the site is explained at the Goonhilly visitor centre, which has lots of exciting interactive displays.

Goonhilly is also a hub for sub-marine cable links, and although its work relating to these cables will continue, its use of the dishes will not. Sadly, as happens sooner or later to all technology, the big dishes of Goonhilly have had their day. In 2006 British Telecom announced that satellite work would move out of Cornwall, taking the dishes with it.

In future years it will seem strange that Cornwall should ever have been chosen as the hub for world-wide telecommunication links, but its geographical position made it the ideal choice for such work. In 1901 Marconi had made radio contact with Newfoundland, and transmitted the first transatlantic broadcast from Poldhu, on the coast of the Lizard peninsula; but geographical location matters less now, and it seems that most of Goonhilly's former functions will be moved to Herefordshire. It is expected that all of the dishes except Arthur will be moved.

Arthur is now a Grade II listed structure, which stands proud over the surrounding heathland environment and is a readily identifiable landmark, visible for miles around. The visitor centre will also remain to remind us of the vital role played by Cornwall in the formation of our modern telecommunication systems.

Gwennap Pit

Right: The concentric circles of Gwennap Pit.
Above: People gather for a service at Gwennap Pit.

In many ways John Wesley (1703–91) was a revolutionary; his approach to religion changed the lives of many and helped to establish Methodism. He visited Cornwall regularly, preaching as often as he could, and the grinding hard lives of the mineworkers made them particularly receptive to his ministry. He preached of the importance of every person to God, and was motivated to improve the lot of workers, particularly through education. His work involved fighting social injustice in all forms. He helped to set up reading groups to improve literacy and to give the poor a foundation for a better life, while also writing a great deal of his own, being involved in around 400 publications.

He must have been charismatic, a superstar of his time: we can imagine people excitedly looking forward to his preaching, desperate to be there.

More than any other location, we associate John Wesley with Gwennap Pit near the mining area of St Day. Gwennap Pit is a circular preaching pit with perfectly symmetrical sloping sides. It might originally have been a natural depression in the ground, or perhaps it was a collapsed early mine working, but either way this pit would have afforded some protection from the winds, and its shape is said to help improve the acoustics.

John Wesley describes the site in his journal as being about 50 feet [15 metres] deep, and perhaps 200 to 300 feet [60–90 metres] across. He was well used to such outdoor venues, and to large crowds. He certainly must have attracted large numbers: he preached at Gwennap Pit on 18 occasions between 1762 and 1789, and in 1781 recorded that as many as 2,000 people had come to hear his sermon. His journal records that it was a calm day, and all could hear him.

After his death, in 1806 the pit was remodelled into its current shape as a memorial to Wesley. Thirteen terraces or levels were created to allow seating, and steps were built leading down to the central depression. The amphitheatre still holds around 2,000 people, and is occasionally used for services today – most notably the Whitsuntide Monday service which has been held here since 1807. More recently a small visitor centre has been added.

All are welcome to come along and imagine the huge crowds standing in a rough pit, straining to hear the words of a man who might be able to change their lives for the better.

Hell Bay

Right: A view of Hell Bay, Bryher.
Above: Waved heath near Hell Bay.

Bryher is a small island at the eastern edge of the Isles of Scilly. It covers 132 hectares and holds a tiny permanent population of around 70 people – a figure regularly boosted by visitors. It is very much an island of contrasts: its eastern edge lies across a sheltered stretch of water from Tresco; to the south are some stunning sandy beaches, none more welcoming than Rushy Bay, but to the north and west it is a different story.

The exposed granite coast of Hell Bay is as awesome a stretch of coastline as any in the South West of England. The land here faces the full force of the Atlantic Ocean. The wind, rain and salt spray have carved wondrous shapes out of the hard granite as if it were as pliant as plasticine. Though such natural sculptures can be found in other parts of the county, there is one subtle difference between the north of Bryher and all other parts of Cornwall and the Isles of Scilly, save the northernmost tip of Tresco.

The rocks and soil of this headland lie in evidence to a very unusual period in the history of the South West. The north end of Bryher marks the most southerly point in the UK that was influenced by ice sheets during the last Ice Age. Recent surveying of this location has pieced together the evidence through analyzing three main factors. Some of the deposits of soil found here are thought to have been brought from further north by the movement of the ice sheet across Ireland. It is thought that some of the large granite boulders on the Down, known as erratics, have been dumped by the movement of the ice and left scattered in ways typical of glaciation. Finally, the granite tors on the headlands to the far north of the island around Hell Bay have been stripped of their uppermost rocks, leading to the suspicion that the ice sheet toppled them off as it ran aground here.

The area known as Shipman Head Down, just inland of Hell Bay, is one of Scilly's best examples of waved heath. Here the heathers and gorse grow so short that bare ground is visible between the plants, and the pattern created is similar to the waves on the nearby ocean. Look around this heathland and you will see evidence of human activity dating back thousands of years. Linear arrangements of stones mark boundaries used by our Bronze and Iron Age ancestors, and circular arrangements of similar stones are often burial mounds. In this one small area there are a staggering 134 such burial mounds, making this the most densely situated collection of archaeological remains in the county.

Its name alone should be enough to conjure up a picture of this wild bay, but there is no substitute for actually seeing it.

Holy Wells

Right: The holy well at St Keyne.
Above: The holy well at Madron, strewn with rags.

Cornwall has many holy wells. There are around 20 in Penwith alone, and it is thought that they have links to Celtic traditions. The trees around the site of Madron Holy Well are strewn with bits of fabric, ribbons and rags; this sort of behaviour can make the place look an unholy mess, so why do we do this to our holy wells?

Madron Well, north-west of Penzance, is close to a Celtic chapel, or baptistery, known as St Maderne's Bed, although the exact identity of St Maderne is unclear. The site is at the end of a footpath, and the well remains unmarked except for a short step down to the water. In fact you might miss the site were it not for the offerings in the overhanging trees.

There are many tales of people who benefited from the water here. In the seventeenth century John Trelille was, reputedly, cured of his crippled state after bathing repeatedly in the water. Others were similarly cured, often after bathing or drinking and then spending a night on St Maderne's Bed (the stone slab in the nearby chapel). It was said that children could be cured of rickets if they bathed regularly during May, and that unmarried women would soon find a spouse if they threw an offering into the well.

In contrast, St Keyne's Well, a few miles north of West Looe, lies next to a road and looks more formal, being sheltered by a protective stone mantle. The life of St Keyne is reasonably well known. She was born in AD 461 in Wales, and travelled widely. St Keyne rejected many proposals of marriage, devoting herself instead to a life of helping and healing others. She reputedly gave this well to the local people, and her blessing conferred on the water an unusual power: for any married couple, whoever first drank the waters held the power within the marriage. This novel idea captured the imagination of the Poet Laureate Robert Southey, who made St Keyne's Well the subject of a poem; in it the bridegroom rushes out of the church to gain the first mouthful, only to discover that his wife took a bottle of well water with her to the church!

The ancient tradition of visiting a holy well and leaving an offering, or seeking a cure, continues to this day. Originally it was believed that if a person was crippled or had an infection, by tying a bandage from the affected part of the body in the trees around a holy well they would be cured. This belief has been interpreted more broadly, so that now people bring any offering to tie up in the hope that it will bring good health.

Holy wells are powerful places; many, like Madron, reputedly have healing qualities; others are linked to legends and rituals. All have an air of mystery about them.

Jamaica Inn

Right: Inside the museum at Jamaica Inn.
Above: Jamaica Inn.

At first thought it seems strange that an inn could be categorized as iconic, but mention Jamaica Inn to almost anyone and it will immediately spark interest. This is probably more a result of the du Maurier novel of that name than a facet of the building itself, though the setting of this inn is the reason for its choice by du Maurier, and the reason why it has such a fascinating history and reputation.

Travellers through Cornwall will have been familiar with Jamaica Inn since it was built in 1750. Today, crossing Bodmin Moor on the A30 is a straightforward journey, but imagine doing so on horseback, on a wet, windswept night. For travellers between Launceston and Bodmin it must have been a most welcome sight, providing shelter and sustenance in an isolated and potentially dangerous spot.

Jamaica Inn had a reputation as a haunt for smugglers, because all of the contraband landed around the coast of Cornwall would have been ferried out of county along this route. It is thought that about a quarter of all the brandy smuggled into Britain was landed around the coast of Cornwall. Surprisingly, tea was another highly smuggled commodity, but it is likely that the healthy trade in Jamaican rum earned the inn its name. Many smuggling and wrecking tales are wishful thinking, but certainly ships were lost, sailors drowned, and cargo wilfully looted and stolen. Altogether enough to get anyone's imagination excited!

Daphne du Maurier stayed at the inn, and experienced the difficulties of Bodmin Moor in bad weather when she and her companion lost their way while out riding. These experiences must have helped shape the novel which tells of a smuggling and wrecking gang based at the inn. The heroine, Mary Yellen, arrives orphaned at Jamaica Inn to live with her aunt. She slowly uncovers the true horror of the evil doings on the moors, and the part played by the inn. Mary realizes too late who the true villain is, and is lucky to be saved from his grasp. The descriptions of the moor surrounding the inn are accurate and realistic; the true horror of wrecking and lawlessness captured in graphic detail. It is this sinister setting which helped to turn *Jamaica Inn* into Daphne du Maurier's first bestseller.

Today Jamaica Inn remains an ideal stopping point on a journey into the county. It provides food and shelter, and features a museum illustrating the history of smuggling in the area and details of du Maurier's life and work.

King Harry Ferry

The River Fal is one of Cornwall's longer rivers, and around its huge estuary a major industry in shipping and maritime interests has developed. One feature of this estuary is that, unlike most estuaries in the rest of the country, it is very deep, even in places where it isn't very wide. This is due to the manner in which it formed.

The name given to this type of estuary is a 'ria'. Rias were initially river valleys which, as anyone who has studied Geography will know, have a V-shaped profile. Since the last Ice Age, Cornwall has seen a rise in sea levels which has effectively drowned the valley of the River Fal. This not only explains the unusually deep water in this estuary, but also the rocky edges and the oak trees that dip their branches into the salt water at high tides.

Such deep water is ideal for the passage of vessels, but not so straightforward for those on foot or wheels. If you happen to be somewhere to the south of Truro and need to get across to the Roseland peninsula then the journey is a long one – up to 40 km. It makes the idea of a ferry extremely attractive.

The King Harry is an attractive ferry in every sense. The ferry itself is unusual as it is one of only five chain ferries still to be found in the country. The setting for this passage is simply stunning, crossing between the wooded valley slopes of the Roseland to the east and Trelissick Garden to the west. There has probably been some sort of ferry crossing here for many centuries, but the King Harry, as we know it, dates from 1888 when the company of the same name was established. It is named after the crossing point and was powered by steam until the mid-1950s, hence the original name of King Harry Steam Ferry.

During the Second World War the ferry was taken over by the military, mostly because the American troops were based in the area preparing for D-Day. General Eisenhower crossed the Fal many times here; in fact, as coal was in short supply during the war, the Americans kept the ferry operational by providing fuel for it.

The current ferry is the seventh and largest of its kind to be used here. It boasts a glass panel so that passengers can see the chain in operation as it crosses the 250-metres stretch of river. The service runs approximately every 20 minutes between Feock and Roseland, and there are now connecting passenger ferries to Falmouth and Truro from Trelissick.

The King Harry Ferry isn't just a ferry; it has been around long enough to have become a part of the Cornish way of life.

Left: King Harry Ferry.
Above: Glass panelling on the ferry.

Kit Hill

Right: The chimney stack on Kit Hill.
Above: Kit Hill.

The position and shape of Kit Hill, near Callington, make it stand out for miles around, and the same two features, along with its geology, have made it the subject of our attention for many millennia. Views from its 334-metres summit are far-reaching, and include Plymouth, Bodmin Moor, and even the countryside around Bude.

We know that Kit Hill was important to Neolithic people because a long barrow dating from between 4,000 and 3,000 BC has been found on the eastern slope. In total there are 18 Bronze Age (*c.* 2000 BC) burial mounds on the hill that we are aware of, and it has obviously been used as a defensive position through the ages. In AD 838 the Anglo-Saxon King Egbert decided to challenge the Cornish resistance, and a battle was fought at nearby Hingston Down in which the Cornish were defeated. To commemorate this battle, Sir John Call built a huge folly on the summit of the hill in the late eighteenth century; the pseudo-fortifications, made to look like a Saxon hill fort, built with this folly are still clearly seen today but are overgrown by grass. The hill's ceremonial function continues to this day, with the lighting of a bonfire at the summit by the Old Cornwall Society on Midsummer's Eve.

It was only really at the beginning of the nineteenth century that the contents of the hill became more important to us than its shape. In about 1820 mining became dominant in the landscape. At first Kit Hill Mine with its wind-powered engine, and then South Kit Hill Mine, which reached a depth of 90 metres, both extracted copper and wolfram from the hill. On the eastern slopes it is easy to see where, as recently as 1918, adits were used to extract wolfram – an element used to harden steel – from close to the surface. Further work on the hill included the quarrying of granite, with its associated inclined railways, the paths of which are still visible on the north side of the hill, but this ended in 1955.

The miners and quarrymen didn't have it all their own way, for when they wanted to erect a stack on top of the hill in 1858 the Duchy of Cornwall, which owned the land, insisted that it should be of ornate design. It is good to see that the shape and position of the hill was still recognized as being of great significance; in fact the stack even acted as a beacon to ships at sea, though it is now smothered in rather ugly modern communications aerials.

Kit Hill was given to the people of Cornwall in 1985 by the Duchy of Cornwall to commemorate the birth of Prince William, which seems fitting as it has been revered by the local inhabitants for so long. Today it is a Country Park managed by Cornwall County Council, which encourages local recreation as well as the conservation of its wildlife and archaeology.

Kynance Cove

*Above: Bloody Cranesbill grows at
Kynance Cove.
Right: Kynance Cove.*

Kynance Cove is one of the most dramatic pieces of coastline imaginable. The geology which has helped to create this coastline has also provided a medium in which an unusual range of wild-flowers can flourish. To top it all there is a tremendous beach which attracts huge interest in the summer.

The geology of the Lizard peninsula is extremely complex – so complex that even the geologists are still debating exactly how it was formed. One thing that everyone agrees about is that it was formed in a different era and in a different part of the world from the rest of the county, being welded on to the Cornish mainland by plate tectonics. The rocks of the Lizard began forming about 375 million years ago. At that time molten rock was forced through the Earth's crust on to the bed of the Rheic Ocean, which then separated Africa and South America from Europe and North America, in the Southern hemisphere.

The most distinctive rock of the Lizard is known as serpentine – a name which came about because its texture was likened to that of a serpent's skin. Serpentine can be found around Kynance Cove, and is most unusual in that it was formed from rock which was originally found extremely deep under the Earth's surface. When in a molten state, serpentine was situated at a depth of at least 10 kilometres below ground level, at the interface between the Earth's solid crust and its liquid mantle.

There are actually two types of serpentine, and both can be found at Kynance. It is thought that the coarser-grained bastite serpentine changed less, as it was forced through the Earth's crust, than the finer-grained tremolite serpentine. Obviously both were put through intense heat and pressure, inducing quite radical changes to their structure. Now the beauty of polished serpentine can be appreciated in the sculptures produced by craftspeople on the Lizard, or at the various points along the Coast Path where it has been polished by the feet of countless walkers.

Serpentine rock is high in magnesium, which has an interesting effect on the flora of the Lizard. One noticeable species in early summer at Kynance Cove is the bloody cranesbill, more typical of limestone areas. Spread around the heaths of this area is a species of heather, the Cornish Heath, which is endemic to the Lizard. On the coast above the cove, look out for the herd of Highland cattle: these have been introduced here to keep the encroaching scrub at bay, to help encourage wildflowers.

Land's End

*Right: Land's End from Pordenack Point.
Above: Land's End from Mayon Cliff,
showing the remains of the* Mulheim.

Land's End is the most westerly point in this country; it is where the British mainland meets the Atlantic Ocean. Embark from here and the next stop is the Americas. Its position alone is sufficient to warrant its inclusion as an icon, and to capture the imagination.

The rock here is granite which forms cliffs that reach to around 70 metres high. These cliffs are pocked by caves and cracks, and eroded to form sea stacks and arches. Walk a little distance from the Land's End complex towards Nanjizal and you will be treated to the spectacular sea stacks and arch of the rocks named Enys Dodnan and Armed Knight.

The rocks here are dangerous, and the site of many shipwrecks, so it makes sense that a lighthouse should be constructed here. The Longships light is about 1.6 km out from the Land's End coast, and was first lit in 1795. Understandably, this was not an easy light to maintain; apparently the original light was often under water as the waves crashed over it. To build here successfully was an amazing feat, achieved by James Douglas who constructed the granite tower we see today in 1875.

Even with a lighthouse, ships are still being wrecked along this part of the coastline. One recent example was the RMS *Mulheim*, which crashed on to rocks between Land's End and Sennen in 2003. Attempts were made to remove its cargo of shredded plastic, but much of it was washed out of the holds and has been deposited on to the sea bed.

The mystery of the deep oceans beyond Land's End has captured imaginations for hundreds of years; many believe that the lost kingdom of Lyonesse lies here. Although legend links this to King Arthur and his heir, Tristan, who was to inherit this kingdom, sadly that is probably a myth. However, it is possible that there was land here at a time when sea levels were lower. Certainly the Isles of Scilly were once part of a larger land mass, which drowned after the end of the Ice Age as sea levels rose. In the legends, the area was said to have been inundated by the ocean shortly after Tristan inherited the kingdom; luckily, he was at the court of his uncle at the time.

Some people come to Land's End to begin the famous 1,600-kilometres journey to John O'Groats, but for the more casual visitor there is a theme park complex to keep you entertained.

Lanhydrock

Right: Lanhydrock House.
Above: Flowerbeds at Lanhydrock.

Lanhydrock nestles gently into the stunning scenery of the Fowey valley. This house – possibly the most splendid in Cornwall – offers an insight into the Victorian Age, so much of the lifestyle of the Victorian aristocratic family is preserved here.

Lanhydrock House was originally a Jacobean mansion which was destroyed by fire and rebuilt in the late nineteenth century. Some of the original house survived, and was incorporated into the Victorian grand design. The estate was originally part of a priory which was destroyed when Henry VIII dissolved the monasteries, and after a series of owners it was bought by Sir Richard Robartes in 1620. Lanhydrock continued as the Robartes' family home until the estate was handed to the National Trust in 1953.

A tour around the house today is like peering back in time: the large nursery suite occupies several rooms on the first floor, demonstrating just how important childhood was in the Victorian age; also on the first floor are the boudoir suites – wonderful fantasy rooms with plump, four-poster beds, and a huge mahogany-trimmed bath for the discerning gentleman. The long gallery is the most spectacular room imaginable. As part of the north wing, its original seventeenth-century plaster ceiling depicting 24 scenes from the Old Testament survived the fire in 1881. David and Goliath are particularly imposing from their position above the entrance. The gallery is home to 3,000 books, all published before 1500, making this the single most historically important area of the house.

A tour of Lanhydrock ends in the 'well-renowned' kitchens, which were totally refurbished in the 1880s using the latest technology available at the time. The sideboards groan with plates and tureens, saucepans and gadgets; there are some wonderfully quirky examples of the latter, such as a glass cockroach trap. The adjacent larders with their marble and slate surfaces demonstrate how it was possible to keep cream and butter in perfect condition before the days of refrigerators. When the family were in London, dairy produce was parceled up and sent to them daily from the nearby station.

The 182-hectare grounds provide a chance to get away from it all, whether walking along the riverbank or wandering through bluebell woods. Closer to the house about 9 hectares of formal garden are a riot of colour in spring, and the flowerbeds cut into the lawns are stunning throughout the summer. There is also a fifteenth-century church in the grounds. Lanhydrock certainly gives you the opportunity to spend a day immersed in the grander side of our history.

Lanyon Quoit

Right: Lanyion Quoit at night.
Above: Chûn Quoit.

A quoit, known in other parts of the country as either a cromlech or a dolmen, is a huge slab of stone lying flat, rather like a table top, supported by several upright stones. This arrangement produces a large stone box or chamber that would once have been used to hold the remains of the dead. It is likely that a quoit would have been the centrepiece of ritual and ceremony, with the larger examples acting as a symbol of power among the Neolithic people who built them. Originally much of the structure of a quoit would have been covered by a mound of soil and stones, with perhaps just the flat capstone and maybe an entrance exposed. Over the last 4,000 years or so, the upright stones of many quoits have become visible largely because surrounding stones and earth have been removed for other purposes.

There are several quoits in Cornwall, with possibly the best preserved being Chûn Quoit. Chûn has an eight-tonne capstone sitting robustly on its original uprights, and though there has been some collapse it is still possible to see the intended structure. Chûn Quoit is situated on high ground near Chûn Castle, far away from any modern roads, so is relatively infrequently visited.

This is in marked contrast to Lanyon Quoit, situated immediately adjacent to a road, and therefore probably the most famous of our quoits. The main stones of Lanyon Quoit, which consist of three uprights and a huge 5-metres-long capstone weighing in at 13 tonnes, appear to be original, but sadly this is not the case. When first built there were four uprights, holding an even larger capstone, but one upright gave way during a storm in the early nineteenth century.

Before its collapse, the quoit was massive: it is said that a man could easily ride his horse through the structure. When it was resurrected, the three remaining uprights were significantly shortened, and the orientation of the capstone was changed. Originally it was aligned north-east to south-west, possibly to line up with other ancient monuments in the area, but now it rests at right angles to this. As a result we are able to marvel at the structure of a quoit and the methods that enabled such a huge stone to be hoisted on to the uprights, but we aren't really viewing a true ancient megalith, and must interpret the remains with caution.

Despite Lanyon Quoit being reinstated in this fashion there is a very special atmosphere about it, which is enhanced by its isolation in this West Penwith moorland setting. It is possible to sit peacefully here and reflect upon the lifestyle of a little understood early Cornish civilization.

Launceston Castle

At one time Launceston was the most important town in Cornwall. It is easy to see the settlement as a significant stronghold since it is sited on a hill and is in close proximity to the River Tamar – a river which must be crossed by anyone entering the county.

If Cornwall is your domain, then it makes sense to protect it at its boundary, hence Launceston Castle was built soon after the Norman Conquest. Possibly this site had served earlier defensive needs; it was important to the Earls of Cornwall, and later held an administrative capacity.

The castle was originally built as an earthwork castle (basically in the motte and bailey style) typical of the eleventh century. The main castle sits on a high mound dominating the landscape, while around it are various ditch-like boundaries.

Although this was the seat of the Earls of Cornwall, it was not until the thirteenth century, when Richard became Earl of Cornwall, that the castle was reinforced. Richard was the brother of Henry III, and an important figure in the political world. He oversaw the strengthening of the castle using stone, and added to it extensively by rebuilding the main tower and gatehouses. This made the castle easier to defend, and provided accommodation for more soldiers.

In the late thirteenth century the administrative centre for the county was moved to Lostwithiel, and Launceston Castle was no longer quite so significant; its role changed to one of court and jail. One of its most famous prisoners was George Fox, founder of the Religious Society of Friends (the Quakers), who was imprisoned here for a few months, during which time he kept a diary of his incarceration. Many were less fortunate, and never saw release. Launceston Castle was the site of many executions or public hangings, the last of which took place in 1821, when the legal functions of Launceston were moved to Bodmin, which had by then become the county town. After this the castle had no specific purpose; sections were demolished, the grounds landscaped, and the area turned into a public park.

However, Launceston Castle does retain significance in the life of the Duke of Cornwall, as it features in the ceremony to proclaim the Duke. The Duchy of Cornwall is an estate owned by the monarch's eldest son. Prince Charles was proclaimed Duke of Cornwall in 1973, and received his feudal dues at Launceston Castle. The dues included a pound of pepper and a pair of white gloves … considerably less valuable than the Duchy of Cornwall estate.

Visiting Launceston Castle is a great way to look back at the administrative history of Cornwall over the last thousand years.

Left: Launceston Castle.
Above: Looking down into the keep.

Lizard Point

Right: Lizard Point is the most southerly point in England.
Above: The chough is an iconic Cornish bird.

The Lizard Point is one of the most famous headlands in Britain because it is the most southerly point on the mainland. It is also home to the first purpose-built wireless station, erected when Marconi located the Lloyds Signal Station here in 1901. Recently, the headland has shot to fame among naturalists as the place where choughs have returned to breed in Cornwall (and England) for the first time in half a century.

The chough is a small crow, similar in size to the jackdaw, but its plumage is glossy black all over and it has a bright red bill and legs. In flight the chough can be distinguished from a jackdaw by its broader wings with splayed 'finger tips', and it rarely flies without making a fuss, so its enthusiastic 'chi-ow' call is quite distinctive.

The chough's association with Cornwall is confirmed by the range of local names that it has been given, including Cornish Jack, Cornish Daw, Cornish Chough and even Market Jew Crow. Though the chough might once have lived in other parts of England, it hasn't bred anywhere else in the country in the last couple of centuries.

The chough was important enough to our ancestors to have been included on the Cornish coat of arms, along with a fisherman and a miner. The link between miner and chough was a stronger one than we might have thought, and the decline in one certainly led to the demise of the other. While mines in the county were active there were many pit ponies grazing the coastal areas. This grazing enhanced the chough's habitat, but as soon as the ponies were removed the chough's demise was signalled. Prior to the start of this century the last choughs to breed successfully in Cornwall did so in 1947. What I find amazing is that the last surviving Cornish bird, born in 1947, is thought to have lived until 1973, reaching a ripe old age of 26!

After a long absence, three choughs accidentally found their way to the Lizard peninsula in 2001, and in 2002 two of the three birds paired up and bred, making this the first breeding record of choughs in Cornwall for over 50 years.

The nest site was cloaked in secrecy, and heavily guarded around the clock by a team of volunteers against the threat posed by egg collectors, and the choughs were successful in raising three young. The following year, watched by the media and the wider public, saw the same pair raise another three young choughs, and their success has continued, reaching a total of 20 young raised in their first five years of breeding. Their chosen nest site, now well known, is in a small cove just to the west of Lizard Point lifeboat station.

Like the choughs, the wireless station has also seen a revival. The building has been restored to its original state, complete with replicas of the equipment used by Marconi all those years ago.

Men-an-Tol is a mystery; it is a unique megalithic monument of which we have no real understanding. The term *men-an-tol* means literally 'holed stone', but this is a stone between two standing stones, and possibly lying within the remains of a stone circle. There is no other such monument within Cornwall, and although other holed stones do exist (most notably on Orkney, close to the Ring of Brodgar), we know of no other in such an arrangement.

The holed stone stands about one metre high, with a hole of about 45 centimetres diameter through the centre. This hole has clearly been worked, and so must have a purpose. Its size means a typical adult can pass through it, but only by crawling on hands and knees. To either side of this the standing stones are about 1.2 metres high, and can be viewed through the hole. Work by the Cornwall Archaeology Unit has shown that there was probably a stone circle on this site, with 19 or 20 upright stones, and there is definite evidence for 11 of these. This stone circle would fit with the pattern of other stone circles found within Penwith, which are situated on high ground, above a height of 100 metres, and contain between 20 and 22 stones, but there is no evidence of any other holed stones.

Inevitably people have tried to discover reasons for this creation. Observations of lunar movements have suggested that the position of the moon may have had an influence on the positioning of the stones, since certain moon rises would have been clearly viewed through the hole from the centre of the circle. Of course this could just be a coincidence, or it could indicate that the circle and stone combination were part of a significant lunar observatory. Other possibilities include that the holed stone was moved here from elsewhere at a later date, or that it was part of a tomb. Part of the charm and excitement of Men-an-Tol is that we just don't know.

The site has become the subject of many local superstitions – most notably the idea that the stone has the power to heal illness. Children could be cured of tuberculosis or rickets if passed naked through the stone three times. Adults could be cured of spinal problems if they passed three times through the hole against the sun. These are just two of the possibilities; there are others concerning fertility and rheumatism, to name but a couple.

Left: Men-an-Tol at dusk.
Above: The holed stone at Men-an-Tol.

Morwenstow is a hidden gem. Situated about 11 kilometres north of Bude it is Cornwall's most northerly parish – an attractive village nestling into a steep-sided valley away from the beaten track. It might have remained hidden and relatively unknown, had it not been for a nineteenth-century vicar who made a name for the village and earned a reputation for himself.

Robert Stephen Hawker was born in 1803 and lived in Morwenstow as a child, but he left the area to study at Oxford. He was ordained a priest in 1831, and took up the rectorship of Morwenstow Church, a Norman church dedicated to St Morwenna and St John the Baptist, in 1834. Despite there having been no vicar in residence at Morwenstow for the previous 100 years, and with the dominance of smugglers and wreckers in the area, he kept his position for the next 40 years until he died.

His approach was, to say the least, eccentric, and must initially have bemused the locals. This opium-smoking vicar was renowned for his odd appearance and habits. He built his own vicarage, was known to have dressed up as a mermaid, and even excommunicated his cat for mousing on Sundays! His most common attire was a fisherman's jersey or 'gansey', which he is reputed to have made himself. It must have endeared him to the fishing community, and he certainly cared for those at sea. He was a man who lived according to his faith, in particular in insisting that any drowned sailors should receive a Christian burial (previously they would have been buried where they were found). He even recovered bodies himself, and so, despite his eccentricities, he was highly respected by his parishioners.

Hawker is credited with introducing the harvest festival service as we know it today, when in September 1843 he held a service using bread made from the first corn to celebrate and give thanks for the successful harvest. This idea soon spread throughout the Victorian church, and must have been appreciated by those working the land in the locality.

Left: The church and vicarage of Morwenstow.
Above: Hawker's Hut near Morwenstow.

One of the National Trust's smallest buildings is the hut that Hawker built on the coast (now known as Hawker's Hut), where he wrote poetry and passed the time in contemplation. He is said to have encountered Lord Tennyson along this stretch of coast, without recognizing the poet. This, and similar meetings, may have helped inspire Tennyson with his *Idylls of the King*, as Hawker was himself an Arthurian expert. Hawker's most famous poem is without doubt *The Song of the Western Men*. Often referred to as *Trelawny*, it tells of the reaction of local men to the imprisonment of Bishop Trelawny by King James II. It is still sung today, and is regarded by many as the Cornish anthem.

Hawker's influence on the church, the people he ministered to, and those of us who love Cornwall is immense, and his life certainly adds colour to the history of Morwenstow.

Mousehole

Right: Mousehole harbour.
Above: The Christmas lights
of Mousehole.

Mousehole has been described as the loveliest village in England, and as such deserves its status as an important Cornish location. What Mousehole also offers is a reminder of some of the best aspects of a Cornish maritime life, and the potential for catastrophe that such a life can hold.

Mousehole appears to be an unspoilt fishing village, with narrow roads and old cottages. However, these old cottages are not as old as they might have been because, with the exception of one house, the whole village was burned to the ground by the marauding Spanish as they ransacked this stretch of coast in 1595. On 23 July 1595, a raiding party of four galleys landed about 600 men from the Spanish Armada, armed with muskets, in Mousehole. The Cornish people, hopelessly out-gunned, fled. The Spanish pillaged and burned houses in Mousehole, Newlyn and Penzance, with Mousehole the worst hit. The situation was corrected when Lord Godolphin called for assistance, and within a couple of days the attack had been repelled. This was the last aggressive invasion of Cornish territory.

Apart from the obvious beauty of the harbour, one of the most notable features of Mousehole is its Christmas lights. In winter the harbour entrance is blocked to protect it from the worst of the weather; then, all around the harbour, across the village and to the hill behind, an array of colourful lights is displayed from mid-December. The lights inevitably draw people from a wide area, as these Christmas decorations light up such a spectacular location.

Winter is a significant time in Mousehole. On 23 December, residents celebrate Tom Bowcock's Eve by eating star gazy pie. Legend has it that when food was scarce and the villagers were close to starvation, because fierce seas made fishing impossible, Tom was able to put to sea during a brief lull, and returned with enough fish to feed everyone. The pie is made with the fish heads sticking out, or gazing to the stars.

The Tom Bowcock story is a legend, but there is no shortage of true bravery in this community whose life has long depended upon the dangerous ocean. The most shocking of recent events occurred in 1981, when the Penlee lifeboat was called to assist the crew of the *Union Star*. The eight men of Mousehole who made up the crew of the *Solomon Browne* lifeboat put to sea on 19 December 1981, braving hurricane-force winds and 18-metre waves in an attempt to rescue the crew of this stricken ship near Lamorna. Against the odds, they were able to take some people off the boat, but just when they were near to completing the rescue they and the people they had collected were lost to the sea. The anniversary of this tragedy is marked each year by turning off the Christmas lights; the Penlee lifeboat house remains as it was that night when its boat put to sea for the final time.

National Maritime Museum

Right: The eye-catching structure of the National Maritime Museum in Falmouth. Above: Inside the museum is a wide range of displays.

Falmouth is Cornwall's largest, and the world's third largest, natural harbour (Sydney and Poole are larger), so it is fitting that the National Maritime Museum should find a home in this Cornish town. It is located close to the working docks, amid the comings and goings of boats. The museum is one of our more recent icons – it opened in 2002 –but already it is highly regarded within the county.

The building is of an attractive design, being dominated by wood. Its tower overlooks Falmouth and its docks, and has distant views of the estuary and the Roseland peninsula beyond. At the other extreme, stairs take you down to the Tidal Zone, which lies below water level so that, particularly at high tide, you can watch the sea life watching you.

Within the main body of the museum are displays that share with us the history of maritime activity from around the world. The main gallery houses a collection of boats, from an early Victorian steam launch that helped to set the fashion for boating parties on the Thames, to the Ventnor hydroplane, a vessel reputedly designed for the Chinese government as a fast suicide craft!

Many of the craft on show are suspended from the ceiling in a vast, impressive gallery, so that they can be viewed from all sides. Best of all, displays change on a regular basis. We can only marvel at how these exhibitions are changed as craft of all types are displayed. Visit often and you build wonderful memories, from the craft that helped win Olympic gold to the bathtub Tim FitzHigham rowed across the English Channel. Most of all, you gain an insight into how boat design has progressed.

The galleries provide a wealth of information, and include sections on the development of weather forecasting and the charting of locations. In each area there are unusual interactive displays and ideas to help visitors to experience some of these past maritime techniques. In Cornwall we are never more than 26 kilometres from the sea, so it is not surprising that there are two galleries dedicated to the development of fishing and coastal activities in the county. Local, renowned maritime figures are recognized, along with the history of the pilchard industry, and even the preparations for the D-Day landings, some of which took place in the county.

Falmouth has a significant maritime history. Since Tudor times it has been home to some of our major ships; it was the embarkation point for many journeys, such as those of the packets, and in 2005 it marked the end of Ellen MacArthur's record-breaking, single-handed round the world challenge, for which she was made a Dame.

Newlyn Harbour

Right: Newlyn harbour.
Above: A catch of dogfish at Newlyn.

With such a long coastline and many natural harbours, it was inevitable that Cornwall would develop a thriving fishing industry. The harbour with the largest catch capacity is that of Newlyn. This harbour also has a reputation for its artists, and is Britain's most important place for measuring sea level.

Newlyn is the location of one of the longest continuous sea-level measuring points, so it has become home to the 'Mean Sea Level' – the datum against which all UK tidal and land height measurements are monitored. Collecting and interpreting such information might seem straightforward, but it isn't just the sea that can change. The land can also rise or sink, and in some parts of the UK (but not Cornwall) the land has been very slowly rising since the last Ice Age, effectively 'bouncing back' after the huge weight of the ice was removed. Taking all of this into account, current research shows that the height of the sea around Cornwall, relative to the land, has increased only very slightly since the early twentieth century, and we know that the size of typical waves is also just a little greater than it was. In contrast, parts of Scotland have lower sea levels as the land there is rising faster. As the twenty-first century progresses, and we enter an uncertain age of global climate change, this monitoring of ocean changes will become increasingly important.

Newlyn doesn't just have the county's largest fish catch, it is also the largest in England. The fishing industry here is important to the local economy, and has been so for many years. At one time, pilchards dominated the catch. Today boats travel further afield, are safer, and have the technology to catch a greater range of fish. To accommodate changes in the fleet, the harbour has been regularly extended. The South Pier was built in 1885, while the North Pier was completed in 1886, and then extended in 1892. Change continues, with developments planned to accommodate the fishing industry of the twenty-first century.

The Newlyn painters, attracted here by the quality of the light, regularly captured the frantic activity of the pilchard fishery, and the appalling conditions and dangers associated with it. This school of painters specialized in social realism, painting the people of Newlyn to show their real lives and hardships. The movement, which contrasted with the idealized style of previous artists, was started by two of its most famous painters, Walter Langley and Stanhope Forbes, in 1882. Several paintings from the Newlyn School form part of the collection in the Penlee House Museum & Gallery in Penzance.

Padstow is a harbour which has proved popular through the ages, and some of its success has been due to its ability to adapt. Now, while maintaining its most significant ancient traditions, it is also able to satisfy the demands of the twenty-first-century tourist.

For thousands of years, travellers passing between France and Ireland are thought to have used the Camel and Fowey valleys as part of their journey, thus avoiding the need to navigate the treacherous sea around Land's End. This path, which starts or ends in Padstow, is now known as the Saints Way, and it traces the footsteps of religious travellers from Padstow to Fowey. The best-known of the saints to visit Padstow is St Petroc, who arrived here in the sixth century, and after whom the town was named. The name 'Padstow' seems to be derived from 'Petroces stow', which literally means St Petroc's holy place. He founded a monastery and was buried here. The parish church, still called St Petroc's, is the official start of the Saint's Way. In the churchyard there is a four-holed Celtic cross by the church door.

Like many Cornish towns, Padstow celebrates the arrival of spring with a pagan festival. The Padstow festival is known as the 'Obby 'Oss, and this must be one of the oldest spring celebrations in existence. The Old 'Oss and the Blue 'Oss both dance the streets of the town on 1 May, as crowds follow their progress until they meet at the maypole as the day draws to a close. The town is decorated with as much greenery as possible, while the revellers sing and dance through the town.

In 1899 a railway was built between Padstow and Bodmin, with access thereafter as far as London Waterloo. The demise of this railway line in 1967 was obviously a setback for people of the area, but the irony is that many more people now use this stretch of line than ever before. The difference is that they do so under their own steam, since the railway line has been converted into a cycle trail that leads to Wadebridge – a distance of 8 kilometres – and beyond. It is estimated that about 300,000 people use this cycle way and footpath each year. The path is great for cycling because it is flat, but it also has wonderful views across the estuary, making it very popular with bird watchers. In Padstow there are now facilities for hiring bicycles to take advantage of this route.

Of course, Padstow is still a fishing port with great character, and it is this that must have attracted Rick Stein to open his first restaurant here in the 1970s, specializing in serving fresh local produce, in particular fish caught by local fishermen. His business and fame have flourished and expanded, with quality local fish remaining at the heart of it.

Left: Padstow harbour.
Above: The Camel Trail near Padstow.

Polperro is one of Cornwall's most attractive small fishing villages, nestling into a niche at the base of the cliffs between Looe and Fowey. Its sheltered and hidden location along a difficult stretch of coastline meant that it was ideally placed to be a major player in one particular Cornish activity. Polperro was renowned for its smugglers.

Smuggling was at its height in the eighteenth century. At this time the British government imposed high taxes on certain goods as part of its efforts to finance the wars in America and France. The taxed goods included luxury items such as spirits, tea and tobacco, but also some more basic goods such as salt. Polperro was a hotbed of smuggling activity for two main reasons: one was location, and the other was personnel.

Polperro is remote, and so would have been difficult to access by land or sea, but it was also well situated to smuggle goods from the island of Guernsey in the Channel Islands, from where the majority of such goods were brought. The smugglers of Polperro were different from many others in that they were extremely well organized. This management most famously came from one man, by the name of Zephaniah Job. He acted as a banker and advisor, and even hired lawyers when the law caught up with the villagers. His co-ordination must have encompassed the whole village, since when John Wesley visited Polperro in 1762 he reported that 'well nigh one and all bought, or sold, un-customed goods'.

The authorities became aware of the situation, and did all they could to catch those involved and stop the contraband getting ashore. The skilled smugglers were able to bring ships ashore in Talland Bay at night without lights, and the illegal cargo would have been spirited away before daybreak. Customs officials were stationed on land and in ships at sea to try to prevent the trade. The custom boat *The Hind* was one of the more successful vessels helping to capture a local smuggling ship, *The Lottery*. This particular encounter was linked to the death of a customs official said to have been shot by local man Tom Potter, who was eventually hanged for murder. This is just one of many tragic deaths linked to the illegal trade, since customs officials shot on sight when smugglers were seen. 'Battling Billy' is said to have been shot dead when found with a load of illegal brandy, but he continued to drive his horses on, into Polperro and straight into the water of the harbour!

Smuggling began to diminish in the early nineteenth century, as the wars ended and the government tightened policing of the smuggling trade. The people of Polperro reverted to their legal work in trades such as pilchard fishing, leaving the gruesome history of illegal activities behind.

Left: Polperro harbour.
Above: The narrow streets of Polperro.

Poltesco

Right: The disused buildings of Poltesco.
Above: A close-up of unpolished
serpentine rock.

Today Poltesco is a hidden, quiet cove, with a small shingle beach, difficult access and a couple of ruined buildings. At first glance it appears to be a place to pass by – after all, Cadgwith seems more interesting and is close. But think again. Poltesco has a fascinating history of industry, which makes it well worth a closer look.

Pilchards were caught from many Cornish coastal villages like Poltesco. Usually in late summer the huge shoals of fish would come towards the shore, sometimes millions of fish in one group. Along the coast 'huers' were positioned to spot the shoals. Such was the importance of this work that at various points around the coast of Cornwall there are still 'huer's huts': good examples can be found in St Ives and Newquay. The huers' job was to act as lookout for these shoals of fish; they would alert the men on the fishing boats with their cries, and guide the nets into position by a kind of semaphore system. They may have used the activities of birds such as gannets to assist them in their search, though such large shoals of fish often occur as an obvious bubbling mass near the surface. The seine nets from the fishing boats were wrapped around a shoal, and the fish pulled back to shore where the task of processing began.

Traditionally pilchards were stacked in barrels in a radiating fashion from the centre of the barrel. Salt was packed around the fish to preserve them, and they were pressed tightly down to exclude air. The fish were then safe to store or export. In the days when a use was found for everything, the abundant oil from the fish was kept for use in oil lamps.

By the mid-nineteenth century, spurred on by the interest shown by Queen Victoria, serpentine had become a highly fashionable product. Queen Victoria and Prince Albert were presented with serpentine vases during a visit to Cornwall in 1846, and later decided to use the stone at Osborne House. For a time serpentine was in huge demand as houses throughout the world installed pillars, fireplaces and other accessories. Factories such as the Lizard Serpentine Factory at Poltesco worked flat out producing architectural pieces. The stone, which is beautifully patterned in red or green, must have looked spectacular, but sadly it proved to be a poor interior investment since serpentine dries out and cracks when subjected to dry heat, so the fireplaces which were sent to hot climates such as India soon began to crumble. That, together with changing fashions, led to the demise of the industry and the loss of the factory. However, it is still possible to see some of the work from the Poltesco factory, because the pulpit at St Peter's church in Coverack is made from serpentine and was donated by the company.

By the start of the twentieth century, the two major industries that had excited Poltesco were closing, and the small cove was becoming a shadow its former self.

Port Isaac

The beauty of Cornwall has often been portrayed on film and television, and Port Isaac is one of several locations in the county that has frequently appeared on the screen. A visit to this small port makes it possible to see why it has captured the hearts of producers and directors over the years.

Port Isaac today is still a fishing port, with boats pulled up in the small harbour, and fresh seafood to be had in the village. The port probably dates from Saxon times, when it was first used to export local produce, including pilchards which were processed and packed here before being shipped out. In the sixteenth century, it was pilchards that formed the mainstay of the local economy, but then Delabole slate from the local quarries was also exported from here; other goods traded include limestone, timber and coal. With all this trading Port Isaac became a thriving and busy village, and this continued until the advent of rail and road transport put an end to much of the harbour's trade.

Left: Port Isaac Harbour.
Above: Filming Doc Martin at Port Isaac.

Perhaps the greatest asset Port Isaac possesses, in attracting tourists and film producers, is its architecture. The winding streets and 'opes', or alleys, around the harbour are packed with eighteenth- and nineteenth-century cottages. Many of these are listed, and exploring this heart of the village is an opportunity to step back in time. The village featured in the Poldark television series in the 1970s, and has been used in films such as *Saving Grace* and *The Nightmare Man*. More recently it has had a starring role as Port Wenn in the television series Doc Martin. As with many filming locations, this brings instant fame, and attracts visitors wishing to see where a favourite programme is created. Not surprisingly, Port Isaac is now a very popular holiday location.

It is difficult to resist watching television programmes set in Cornwall because, even if the storyline isn't very good, there is usually some spectacular scenery. This is certainly true of the Port Isaac area, where the coastline is dramatic. To the west, and a reasonable walk away, is the tiny hamlet of Port Quinn. Tiny it may be, but it is a surprise that this hamlet exists at all, given that it has been abandoned twice in its history: once when the pilchards failed and the inhabitants were left without a source of income, and even more tragically, again when all the men were drowned at sea.

Porthcurno

Right: Performing at the Minack Theatre.
Above: Porthcurno Beach with the distant Logan Rock.

This small and unpretentious section of the Cornish coast has more claims to fame than most. It is home to an important piece of communication history; possesses a theatre like no other, and offers probably the most stunning beach in the county, backed by a headland with a history.

The Minack Theatre nestles into the cliff top so that the audience, seated on a rocky slope, faces a stage backed by the open sea. It was built in the 1930s by Rowena Cade, starting out as a project in her back garden but developing and growing into a renowned auditorium. What a wonderful vision she possessed: this amphitheatre is an amazing place to watch performances, and must be an inspirational place to perform. Today the theatre runs a season of performances from May to September, and a visitor centre charts the history of the place.

Before the theatre was conceived, this was already a centre of communication, as Porthcurno was the point at which, in 1870, telegraph cables connecting Britain to India came to land. From here the network expanded, and the telegraph company based its operations at Porthcurno, so that the world's largest cable station developed here in this small Cornish cove. The significance of the station to world communications came to the fore in wartime, and in both World Wars soldiers were stationed here as protection. During the Second World War local miners excavated tunnels into the cliff, and a telegraph station was constructed underground, safe from enemy bombs. Today this is part of the Porthcurno Telegraphy Museum, which provides a fascinating insight into the history of communications before computers and satellites linked us all together.

When visiting Porthcurno, a walk along the Coast Path to the east is irresistible. Here there are not only great views over the beach and of the Minack Theatre, but this is also where the famous Logan Rock is situated. This huge granite boulder was at one time finely balanced here, and could be gently rocked with very little pressure. Understandably, this was a tourist attraction, and held in great esteem by the locals until a certain Lt Goldsmith of the Royal Navy and his crew from HMS *Nimble* thought it would be a good idea to push the rock off the cliff, causing it to crash down to the sea below.

This horrific act of vandalism caused huge offence. It was decided that Lt Goldsmith, with the help of the Navy, should replace the rock. Replace it they did, but it took 60 men some seven months, and cost over £130 to achieve. Since Logan Rock was replaced in 1824 no one has dared to try to loosen its hold on the cliff top. It still rocks, but not as readily as it did.

Restormel Castle

Left: Restormel Castle.
Above: The entrance to Restormel Castle.

It is possible to look down on Restormel Castle from the hills surrounding the Fowey Valley and marvel at the strong circular walls dominating the landscape. Anyone approaching the castle would have been faced with extremely steeply sloping grassy banks, a moat and impregnable stone walls. Viewed from above, the grass and stone are seen to be arranged in concentric circles.

This imposing structure seems even more impressive when you realize that it has been unoccupied and therefore decaying since the sixteenth century. It is located close to the River Fowey, and afforded its inhabitants views across the surrounding countryside. The original building is probably Norman, and may be linked to the time when the river was bridged; certainly it would have offered protection to the river crossing. In 1299 the castle passed into the hands of the Crown as it became the property of Edmund Earl of Cornwall, and it has remained in the possession of the Earldom or the Duchy ever since.

The remains we see today date from around 1300, and follow a fairly typical motte and bailey (mound and walls) style. How incredible that so much survives: the circular tower is about 38 metres in diameter, and the walls were built approximately 2.4 metres thick. The walkway at the top of the wall is still intact, and inside it is possible to see the layout of many of the rooms, including the great hall. The unusually large 17-metres-wide moat is cut into rock rather than just being the result of earth excavation to form a mound. This moat would have been a deterrent to would-be attackers, not only because of its structure, but also because it contained the sewage and garbage of the inhabitants of the castle.

The building of the castle was probably carried out by Richard Earl of Cornwall around the time he moved the administrative centre for the area from Launceston to Restormel, or Lostwithiel. This castle, with its surrounding deer park, certainly reflected the high status of the area, and was the home of the Black Prince for a short while in the middle of the fourteenth century.

By the fifteenth century, the castle had started to fall into ruin, although it received a new lease of life during the Civil War when a garrison of Parliamentary troops held it under the command of Lord Essex. However, the forces of Charles I captured the castle in August 1644.

Roche Rock

Right: The chapel on Roche Rock.
Above: The view down from the top of Roche Rock.

Among the granite areas of Cornwall we find tors. These mounds of granite resist erosion and stand up tall, punctuating the landscape with their jagged outlines and stone piles. One of the most famous of such tors is the Cheesewring close to Minions, but Roche Rock has a particularly unusual profile because, built into the top of this particular granite outcrop, is a chapel which appears to occupy the whole surface of the rock.

This small chapel was built during the early fifteenth century, reputedly by a hermit. This hermit lived here at the apex of Roche Rock, while his daughter daily trekked up and down carrying his vital supplies. The chapel is dedicated to St Michael the Archangel, from whom we get Michaelmas, which is celebrated on 29 September.

It is possible to walk up to the base of the chapel; the view across the surrounding area is stunning, and worth the effort. Looking either from or up to the rock it is clear to see why this place came to be associated with so many myths and legends. There are, after all, few such upstanding vantage points in the landscape.

Perhaps the most romantic of these stories concerns the lovers Tristan and Isolde, of Arthurian legend. Tristan inadvertently shared a love potion with Isolde, who was intending to marry his Uncle Mark. The potion took a strong hold and the pair fell hopelessly in love, much to Mark's annoyance. Tristan and Isolde were forced to hold secret meetings, often pursued by Mark. The lovers found refuge in the small chapel on Roche Rock. It is possible that this is also the location for Tristan's famed leap, as he plunged from a rock to avoid Mark's troops.

It is also said that the Cornish giant, Tregeagle, had the misfortune to get his head stuck in a chapel window here when he was searching for a place to escape the hell hounds. Understandably, he was furious, and bellowed long and loud before finally being freed. On a stormy night it is still possible to hear his eerie calls filling the surrounding countryside. But visitors to Roche Rock shouldn't worry about this particular giant, as he was banished to the Lizard where he was given the unenviable task of collecting all the sand from the beaches!

Smuggler's Cottage

Right: Smuggler's Cottage.
Above: Shipping paraphernalia at Smuggler's Cottage.

Many of the Cornish icons in this book are places that dominate their surroundings – places which we can all identify and locate – but a few are hidden and less well known. Smuggler's Cottage at Tolverne is one such spot, for although it is close to Truro as the crow flies, it has always been a difficult place to get to, unless you know how.

This fifteenth-century thatched cottage nestles into the eastern bank of the River Fal on the Roseland side of the King Harry Ferry. The two means of travel to Smuggler's Cottage are by ferry (from Truro, Falmouth or Trelissick Gardens), or by road (using the King Harry Ferry from the west, or on a long and difficult journey via Tregony from the east). Of the two, it is the ferry trip which seems more appropriate, since this cottage has been an important ferry point since it was built.

There are many cottages on the Fal Estuary whose history is of interest, but Smuggler's Cottage has one element in its past which makes it unique in Cornwall.

The county of Cornwall did not suffer the worst effects of the Second World War; there were some incidents of bombing, such as when Falmouth docks were badly hit in 1940, but that doesn't mean that the county didn't have a positive impact on the war effort. In fact, Cornwall was at the centre of the war effort for a critical period, though not many people knew about it because it was necessarily a well-kept secret.

Smuggler's Cottage was chosen as an embarkation point for American troops in the D-Day landings. The elements which made this place suitable for its chosen purpose were its position on the Fal and its relative isolation. Smuggler's Cottage was chosen for this purpose in 1942, so that between then and 1944 it could be prepared. During that time the area was developed by the American Navy, and though much of their handiwork has been removed, some of it can still be seen. The road to the cottage was made by them, as was the slipway into the river. Along the road we can see the points at which the troops were accommodated, and even the positions of the old sentry posts.

In the build up to D-Day, General Eisenhower, Supreme Allied Commander, was based at the cottage, using it as his headquarters. On the day, 6 June 1944, 27,000 American troops from Cornwall landed on the beaches of Normandy. The troops based at Tolverne were all destined for Omaha beach.

Today, Smuggler's Cottage is a thriving restaurant and tea room. As well as enjoying good food and drink here, visitors can view the many artefacts commemorating the war and explaining the role this building played in it.

Rock has developed into one of the more popular Cornish holiday destinations, and it is easy to see why this town has attracted so much interest. It lies opposite Padstow on the Camel Estuary, and is blessed with a wonderful beach stretching along the estuary and around to Daymer Bay. This peaceful and sheltered sandy stretch is particularly attractive on a warm summer's day, and typifies what Cornwall is about for many people: the chance to relax close to the sea.

The sea may provide a host of leisure pursuits, but it is not without danger, as is demonstrated by the relatively recent creation of a lifeboat station at Rock. Established in 1994, this station covers the Camel Estuary and surrounding waters, initially with an inshore boat. The new lifeboat house was built in 1997, and now houses the small but manoeuvrable D-class boat.

Inland of the Coast Path is an extensive dune system which conceals one of Cornwall's more interesting churches, that of St Enodoc. This is said to be the site of a cave where St Enodoc the hermit lived. The church dates back to at least the fifteenth century, and possibly earlier. One of the problems of building among sand dunes is that the sand does not stay still and, as a result, the church here was buried in sand at some point during the eighteenth or nineteenth century, and fell into disrepair. Yet even when the church was part buried under sand it was still used occasionally, because some ingenious soul created a door in the roof so that the clergy and congregation could gain access. Thankfully, in the mid-nineteenth century renovations took place under the guidance of the vicar, the Revd Hart Smith; sand was removed, sections rebuilt, and a new roof added.

Many people make the one-mile walk across the dunes from Rock, or a slightly shorter path from the car-park in Daymer Bay, to visit the church, because this is the final resting place of the former Poet Laureate Sir John Betjeman. Betjeman spent many years in Cornwall, often referring to his love of the county. He died at Trebetherick, close to Rock, in 1984, and is buried at St Enodoc church. His simple grave is close to the south side of the church, in a peaceful and beautiful spot from where it is possible to sit and admire the view over Daymer Bay towards the open ocean.

Left: St Enodoc Church.
Above: The grave of Sir John Betjeman.

St George's Island (Looe Island)

*Right: The Island House,
on St George's Island.
Above: Jetty Cottage, St George's Island.*

Many of us, at some point in our lives, dream of life on an island; most of us leave it as just a pleasant fantasy, but for Evelyn Atkins and her sister Babs the dream became a reality, and an adventurous one at that. In 1964, the sisters bought St George's Island, just off the coast at Looe, and remained there until they died. The excitement of their lives is captured by Evelyn (known as 'Attie' to her friends) in her two books: *We Bought an Island* (1976) and *Tales from a Cornish Island* (1986). Their story is important, not just because these indomitable women coped with a remarkable lifestyle, but also because on her death Babs left the island to the Cornwall Wildlife Trust, which means that now we can all benefit from her legacy.

St George's Island lies half a kilometre off the coast of Hannafore, near West Looe, and covers just over 9 hectares, with a circumference of about a kilometre and a half. Apart from the Isles of Scilly this is the largest inhabited island off the Cornish coast. In former times it was farmed, particularly for rabbits, and passed between various owners, although for many years it was part of the Trelawny estate. Despite its close proximity to the mainland, it can be extremely difficult to land here – not that Attie and Babs were deterred by such difficulties. Their former house has photographs showing part of their move, with furniture piled precariously and tied on to a boat. Attie chronicles stories of these difficulties, such as the landing of several hundredweight of coal which was promptly washed out to sea by a severe storm, with a sense of humour. She spent days combing the island beaches retrieving lumps of coal! When Babs was teaching at Looe Secondary School, she could only contact her sister by waving from Hannafore Point opposite the island – or with a flashlight at night. Once the weather was so bad that Attie was alone between Christmas and Easter, as Babs was unable to get out.

The Atkins sisters decided to share their island, and were happy to welcome visitors. Initially they thought of setting a landing fee (of 2/6d, or 12½p) to deter craft from landing unnecessarily; but people were more than happy to pay. Attie and Babs ran a small café on the island, serving island jam or luncheon meat sandwiches to guests. As time went on, guests became volunteers – often young people taking the Duke of Edinburgh awards – and they helped to run the island. Evelyn died in 1997, but Babs remained here until her own death in 2004, cared for by two friends who came to live on the island with her.

St Mawes & Pendennis Castles

Right: St Mawes Castle at night.
Above: Pendennis Castle.

The 38-year reign of King Henry VIII, from 1509 to 1547, was tumultuous in many ways. He is probably best remembered for his matrimonial difficulties and religious changes; but the first half of the sixteenth century was also one of military campaigns and battles. Mostly these concerned the French, and it was the threat of a Catholic French- or Spanish-led invasion that prompted Henry to build a series of coastal fortifications in southern Britain. Many of them survive today, but two of the most interesting are the pair built astride the mouth of the Fal Estuary at St Mawes and Pendennis, which were constructed between 1540 and 1545.

The castles were built at the same time, but are not identical. Pendennis is the larger of the two; St Mawes is perhaps the more attractive. St Mawes Castle is shaped like a clover leaf, which allows a greater number of points for gun and cannon placements. Clearly the castle was built to fulfil its military function, but also with an eye for aesthetics; it is an excellent example of Tudor architecture. It is highly decorated, with stone carvings adorning the walls, and is well planned: for example, the gun platforms were built with ventilation shafts to disperse the smoke.

One drawback with St Mawes castle is that it is built on the side of the hill, so while it commands the estuary it would be vulnerable to attack from land. Pendennis sits on top of a hill, giving it dominance to land and sea. So although Pendennis Castle is relatively plain, perhaps it was potentially of a little more use.

As it happens there was no invading force during Henry's reign, but these castles were still highly valued, and both were improved by Elizabeth I following the Spanish raid on Penzance in 1595. The two castles were never used to repel a force from overseas, but they did see some action in the Civil War. The Royalist commander at St Mawes realized the vulnerability of the castle to a land attack, and surrendered to the Parliamentarian forces. Across the estuary, the situation at Pendennis was rather different, and here the Royalists held out against a six-month siege in 1646. The castle was attacked by both land and sea, but proved impregnable to the Roundhead forces and was one of the last fortresses to hold out for the King, capitulating eventually due to lack of food.

Both castles were called into service again during the Second World War: after all they do look out over one of the world's most impressive and significant harbours. Today, both are open to the public, giving us the chance to view the work of one of this country's most interesting monarchs.

St Michael's Mount

St Michael's Mount is quintessentially Cornish; a stunningly beautiful, spectacular coastal location with a wealth of historical interest.

This island, in Mount's Bay, is only a few hundreds metres from the shore at Marazion, and is attached by a causeway which is exposed at low tide. Visitors to the island have a choice of walking when tides are low, or travelling by boat when they are high. The tiny island alone would be interesting, but as it is topped by a castle and steeped in history, it is compelling.

In ancient times, the island is thought to have been a significant port for the export of tin and copper. The history of the buildings that we see today dates from the twelfth century, when Bernard of Le Bec, Abbot of Mont St Michel in Normandy, built a Benedictine priory here. The French continued to oversee the monastery until Henry V declared war on France and seized the island as the property of the enemy; the monastery continued until the time of Henry VIII when, along with many others, it was dissolved.

Left: The causeway to The Mount.
Above: St Michael's Mount.

After that time the Mount took on garrison duties, and was fortified against Spanish and French attacks. The only military action seen here was during the Civil War, when initially the Mount was a Royalist stronghold, but eventually was forced to capitulate to the Parliamentarian forces in 1646. The castle then became home to the St Aubyn family (it was bought by John St Aubyn in 1660), and the buildings were converted into a house. The St Aubyn family passed the ownership of the Mount to the National Trust in the mid-twentieth century, but continue to live there.

Part of the mystery surrounding the site comes from its inaccessibility. Not surprisingly it is associated with many legends, and was once said to be the home of Cormoran, a mythical giant who terrorized the area before he was eventually slain and buried on the Mount. Certainly, a giant would make short work of the path up to the castle door. The steep slopes on the seaward side of the Mount are now the location of a spectacular sub-tropical garden, with many unusual plants growing in this almost frost-free environment.

St Michael's Mount is a fascinating and romantic location, but perhaps it is most significant as a characteristic landmark visible from all around Mount's Bay, which was named because of the presence of this, possibly the most iconic, Cornish icon.

St Piran's Chapel

Right: A re-enactment on the St Piran's Day march.
Above: A Cornish flag flies at the site of the original oratory.

St Piran is the patron saint of Cornwall. He is said to have come to Cornwall from Ireland after locals, jealous of his popularity and healing skills, threw him over a cliff in a storm with a millstone around his neck. As soon as Piran hit the water the storm ceased, and he floated to Cornwall on his stone. The saint is reputed to have landed in the county near to Perranporth at Perran beach, hence the name.

Piran built his original oratory at this site, and began his ministry. There is a very early Christian chapel (*c*. seventh century) on this site, and its dimensions and layout resemble those of Irish oratories of the same period. Sadly, the sand dunes encroached on the building, rendering it unusable (during the eleventh or twelfth century), and in 1980, after many years of sand increasing, being removed and encroaching again, the building was buried to protect it from further damage, and a plaque placed on the site. Many believe that Piran is buried here – there are burial sites in the vicinity. Hopefully, one day the oratory can be cleared of sand and fully protected for us to view.

A second church dedicated to St Piran was built slightly to the east, but since this was also on the dunes it too became inundated, and in 1805 had to be abandoned. In contrast, the ruins of this chapel are exposed, and the site is protected. Today the St Piran's Day play and procession are held at Perran Sands each year on 5 March, since this is thought to be the anniversary of his death. Both the original oratory and the subsequent chapel form part of the route, as does the ancient holed cross adjacent to the church. It is wonderful to see the black and white flags, which are also a legacy of St Piran, being carried across the sand dunes. The reason for the flag's pattern is that St Piran is said to have found tin when a stone overheated and the tin flowed out to form the shape of a white cross against a black background. As the procession across the dunes progresses, scenes recalling Piran's life and importance to Cornwall are re-enacted; those taking part carry daffodils and lay them to commemorate Piran and his ministry.

Stone Circles

Cornwall has in excess of 30 stone circles in various states of completion, confirming that the county was important to Bronze Age dwellers, and that stone circles held a very significant place in their societies. It is difficult to choose just one stone circle, since there are impressive and well-preserved circles across the county from the Nine Maidens in West Penwith to Nine Stones near St Breward. The circles are most common on Bodmin Moor and in Penwith.

On Bodmin Moor alone there are 15 stone circles, the most well known of which is probably the Hurlers, close to the Cheesewring; here there are three separate circles of stones. Legend has it that the Hurlers were men turned to stone for throwing, or hurling, balls on the Sabbath. This site is especially interesting as remnants of settlements and cairns can also be found in the area. A similar story is linked to the stone circle called the Merry Maidens, near Lamorna in West Penwith. Here 19 maidens are said to have been turned to stone for dancing on the Sabbath. This circle is believed to be complete, which makes it quite unusual. It is about 23.8 metres in diameter, with the tallest stone about 1.4 metres high.

The stone circle at Duloe, near Looe, is intriguing because it is the smallest in the county, with a diameter of less than 12 metres. Part of the intrigue attached to this circle is that we don't know why it is so small, or why it was created here. The Revd Bewes oversaw restoration work at the site in the mid-nineteenth century, when a hedge that had been built across the circle was removed. Although this work restored the stone circle so that it could be enjoyed by all, it also resulted in the breaking of one of the stones. At the same time, one of the Victorian workmen is said to have put a pick through an urn containing bones, suggesting that this might have been a burial site. Sadly, the urn disintegrated, and nothing survived.

The eight stones of Duloe stone circle are very rich in quartz (the only stones of this nature used to build stone circles in Cornwall), and were probably brought from a site near Herodsfoot about 3 kilometres away. This may be a small circle, but the individual stones probably weigh around nine tonnes each, so the site must have had great significance for those involved in its construction.

Left: The Merry Maidens stone circle.
Above: Duloe stone circle.

Tamar Bridges

Right: A rainbow over the Tamar Bridges.
Above: The road and rail bridges over the Tamar.

The River Tamar forms the border between Cornwall and Devon, and has done so since Saxon times. The river has a surprisingly long course, as it rises just 6 kilometres from the Bristol Channel and then flows for 98 kilometres until it reaches the sea at Plymouth Sound. Getting across the Tamar from Plymouth to Cornwall would once have involved a ferry crossing to Torpoint, but in bad weather a long journey by road would have been necessary. All that changed in the nineteenth century, thanks to the genius of one of the country's greatest ever engineers.

The rail bridge, or Royal Albert Bridge, is one of Isambard Kingdom Brunel's masterpieces. It was opened in the year of his death, 1859, and is an outstanding memorial to this wonderful engineer. The bridge is not only beautiful, with its sweeping curves and spans; it is also a triumph of design. The bridge crosses the river at a height of around 30 metres, which allows ships to navigate the waterway at high tide, and consists of two spans each around 137 metres across. Work began in 1849, when Brunel started investigating how to span such a large distance, and how to support the bridge under 21 metres of water and another 4.5 metres of mud and clay.

He eventually decided on two spans which had to be built on land, floated out into the river and then lowered on to their piers through the effect of the tide receding. The tubes and towers of the bridge are intricately constructed, with a series of braces and struts which give the bridge a tremendous stability and weight-bearing ability. In many ways it resembles the principles of a suspension bridge, and it is still the only bridge of this kind to carry a railway line. Brunel's attention to detail is a triumph, as massive locomotives have rolled over his bridge for more than 140 years.

If the rail bridge was necessary to open Cornwall to greater rail traffic, then a road bridge would help further in lessening the county's isolation; but it took another 100 years to build such a road crossing, with the Tamar Suspension Bridge carrying the A38 being completed in 1961. The suspension bridge is just upstream from the Royal Albert Bridge, and was always intended to be a toll bridge to cover the construction costs. Unlike rail travel, the use of motor vehicles has steadily increased, meaning that by the end of the twentieth century the volume of traffic was outstripping the capacity of the bridge. Work completed in 2002 added extra support and a further lane to the bridge, to supplement its weight-bearing ability and reduce congestion.

Many of the buildings that we feel most deeply about are ancient. It almost seems that the older a building is the more we revere it; churches, stately homes, even old cottages are often high up on such a list. Modern architectural creations often generate a negative reaction among the general public. For an example of this we need look no further than the 'new' County Hall building in Truro, which despite being listed has not been selected for this book as an icon of Cornwall.

There are some exceptions to the rule. One building which is modern but has received positive attention is the Tate St Ives. This smooth, white, three-storey building was completed in 1993, transforming the site of an old gas storage tank and bringing a touch of the Mediterranean to the shore of Porthmeor beach. The columns and rotunda set the scene for the space and light that this building brings to its gallery areas. Stand in the circular entrance to the gallery on a stormy day, and you will feel that the waves are breaking around your ears; the design of this feature helps to make the building a part of its wider environment. Of course, not everyone loves this building, but for many it is the architecture which makes a visit to Tate St Ives extra special.

Inside the gallery are permanent collections of work by artists of the St Ives School, including Bernard Leach whose pottery was created in St Ives. St Ives is noted for its artists: they are attracted by the character of the town and by the wonderful light which is often found here. The character is created by the narrow winding streets; the harbour and its boats; the beaches; the steep, stepped pathways, and the artists themselves, through the numerous smaller galleries scattered throughout the town. The exceptional light is a result of sunlight being bounced off many reflective surfaces, including the pale sandy beaches, the white houses, the sea and the blue sky.

Barbara Hepworth's work is intrinsically linked to West Cornwall and the landscape that inspired much of her sculpture. Her abstract forms explored the natural landscape around her. She lived in St Ives from 1949 until her death in 1975; her house is now a museum and part of Tate St Ives. Here it is possible to visit her studio and garden, which contain many of her absorbing pieces in an intimate setting.

Left: The foyer of the Tate Gallery.
Above: The Tate Gallery, St Ives.

Tintagel

Right: The remains of Tintagel Castle.
Above: The headland of Tintagel.

The castle clinging to the rugged cliffs on the north Cornish coast at Tintagel is real enough, but many of its reputed inhabitants are shrouded in legend. The castle we see today was built in 1233 for Richard Earl of Cornwall, brother to Henry III, and his choice of location may have been linked to the stories of King Arthur's presence here. His stronghold was built at the very edge of the headland, but sadly the building was much neglected for periods since that time, and has been in ruins for many years.

These remains may not link to Arthur, but archaeological work on the island adjacent to the headland has shown evidence of habitation from at least the fifth century, and possibly earlier. An inscribed slate is thought to be around 1,500 years old, and tells us that it was made for someone called Artognou. No one knows who this refers to, but it suggests that we are probably looking at a significant location. This island would have been an ideal base for the Celts, and may well have been home to the kings of Dumnonia (Cornwall, Devon and parts of Somerset in the fifth and sixth centuries), the only access being a short bridge from the headland, easily guarded and fortified, and an ideal place for a leader with endeavor and ambition. Possibly this is how it came to be linked with Arthur.

The legends of King Arthur were initiated by Geoffrey of Monmouth in his *History of the Kings of Britain* in 1135. His writings were based on the evidence available at that time, and perhaps embellished a little. These tales were later reworked by Sir Thomas Mallory and others. Arthur was probably a Celtic warrior, and leader in the battles against the Saxons, but there is really no evidence for the existence of many other characters, such as Merlin. Geoffrey describes Camelot as being high above the sea and surrounded by water: clearly Tintagel! Certainly Cornwall was a Celtic stronghold, and the area did hold out against the Saxons for many years, so there were battles in many parts of the West Country, and Tintagel would have been a sensible place to create a safe base.

Tintagel Castle may be in ruins, but it is worth visiting to see the remains of the fortifications and the impressive nature of this coastline. Many do come here to see what they believe is the home of a romantic warrior; his beautiful but adulterous wife; his worthy knights, and the magic of his advisers. There may be no hard evidence of this, but visiting Tintagel allows us to hold on to the great Arthurian legend.

Tors of Bodmin Moor

Right: Granite rocks strewn on Roughtor.
Above: The Cheesewring is a
characteristically shaped tor.

Bodmin Moor covers around 18,220 hectares, making it the largest area of moorland in Cornwall. It was formed about 300 million years ago, when molten rock welled up from the centre of the Earth and solidified at its crust. This intrusion formed a very hard rock which we now know as granite, and because of granite's low permeability and high resistance to weathering, the moor now stands tall above the surrounding landscape.

The highest point on Bodmin Moor is Brown Willy, rising to a height of 420 metres. The majority of us see Brown Willy as we pass on the A30, its series of jagged pinnacles being easy to spot. Close by is the more accessible Roughtor (pronounced 'row' – as in argument), which at 400 metres is a little shorter than its near neighbour, but is a great place from which to admire the wilderness of the moorland.

A tor is a pinnacle of exposed granite, often situated at the very summit of a hill. Tors are formed through a process of weathering by the actions of wind, rain and temperature changes. The most significant weathering probably happened during the last Ice Age. During that time, though Cornwall was not actually covered by ice sheets and influenced by glaciers, it was affected by extremely variable, often very cold, conditions, meaning that for long periods of time the ground was fluctuating between being frozen and thawed. These conditions meant that frost-shattered rock from the peaks was carried off the very tops of the moors by a fluid mixture of mud, rock and water, leaving only the solid rock in place. The hard rocks that withstood the Ice Age have since been sculpted into the wonderful shapes that we now see around Bodmin Moor. The boulders that slipped from the summits during the Ice Age – known collectively as 'clitter' – can now be seen scattered across the moorland.

In the south-east of Bodmin Moor, near the Minions, is found one of the most characteristic of all of the Cornish tors. The Cheesewring looks like a great pile of flattish boulders carefully placed on top of each other. In fact one legend suggests that this is how it was formed! It is said that the saints and giants in Cornwall were in dispute, and in the end decided to have a contest of strength. St Tue represented the saints, and Uther the giants; it was agreed that if the saints lost the contest they would leave Cornwall, whereas if the giants lost they would convert to Christianity. The trial was all about throwing stones, and for each bolder that Uther pitched, St Tue was able to pick a similar or even bigger one, and throw it to land on top of the giant's stone. Their contest created the Cheesewring, and as Uther missed with his last stone it also led to the conversion of the giants.

Trebah Garden

Cornwall boasts an incredible number of fascinating gardens. The location of our county is conducive to plant growth – the maritime conditions and warm, damp climate give rise to a lush growth not easily equalled at 55°N. Our gardens can seem particularly impressive when you realize that places like Kiev in the Ukraine, or Newfoundland in Canada, are on similar latitudes, and in winter typically experience temperatures of around -10°C, while in South Cornwall it is likely that we will be 20°C warmer. No wonder plants thrive here; many have enough warmth and moisture to grow all year round.

At Trebah we also have a valley dipping down to an estuary, sheltered from the worst of the winds and frosts, which opens up on to a breathtaking view, creating the setting for a garden of sublime proportions. Trebah Garden, near Mawnan Smith, occupies 10.5 hectares in one of several small valleys running down to the Helford River. There can be no debate that the setting is beautiful; what was needed was a garden designer who could think big.

Fortunately, in the middle of the nineteenth century, the house and land was owned by Charles Fox. He took on the role of laying out the garden, and his approach to garden design was thorough if a little novel. Before planting each tree the gardeners had to construct a tower with a flag on top, so that Charles could check the tree's final height and position from the windows of the house. His approach paid off, and created a vista of magnificent proportions. Later, Charles' daughter Juliet and her husband Edmund Backhouse added many rhododendrons to the garden.

A great many varieties of plants thrive here. There are several tree ferns, which are over 100 years old and originated in Australia; they live in an environment alongside agaves from the deserts of Central America, aloes from Africa and *Trachycarpus fortunei* (palms) from China. Don't miss the bamboo collection – some grow centimetres each day; or the Gunnera garden, where the leaves of this Brazilian rhubarb grow up to 2.5 metres across. One of my favourites is the tremendous handkerchief tree (*Davidia involucrata*), whose showy white flowers resemble floppy handkerchiefs hanging out to dry. It is hard to know which section is the most impressive sight, or where to look first.

By the middle of the twentieth century, the house and gardens had been bought and sold many times, and the gardens sadly neglected. This is too common a story, as once-great gardens became overgrown and lost. Fortunately for us, in 1981 Trebah was eventually taken on by Tony and Eira Hibbert, who realized what a treasure lay beyond their windows and embarked on restoration – not quite the quiet retirement they had planned! Today the gardens are once again magnificent, with colours and plants to delight at all times of year, a true testament to this amazing location where plants from across the globe can live together.

Left: Trebah Garden.
Above: Flowers of the handkerchief tree.

Treffry Viaduct

Right: The Treffry Viaduct.
Above: Leat and path in the
Luxulyan Valley.

Within our county are several outstanding feats of engineering; most are proudly obvious, and often still in use, but hidden away in mid-Cornwall is an engineering achievement that deserves greater fame. Treffry Viaduct, built as part of the mining industry's nineteenth-century expansion, is an affirmation of the ambition and success of the period. Located just over 6 kilometres from St Austell, this structure towers over the Luxulyan Valley.

The viaduct reaches to about 30 metres high, and measures almost 200 metres long; each of its ten arches spans over 12 metres. The building of this viaduct was a massive undertaking. It is estimated that the amount of granite used in its construction amounted to about 5,660 cubic metres. It is astonishing to think that the whole viaduct, the first of stone construction in Cornwall, was completed in only three years back in 1839. It was an amazingly advanced engineering project in its day, but it is no longer obvious why such a large bridge was ever required in this quiet and tranquil wooded valley. The truth is that this valley was not always peaceful; it was once a hive of industry.

Joseph Treffry had ambitious plans for this area; he inherited the land in 1813, and set about exploiting its mineral potential. The viaduct is actually a small part of the empire he constructed, which included the harbour at Par, a canal and a railway; he had even acquired the port of Newquay, and was planning railway links to the town to encourage visitors.

The Treffry Viaduct is part of the railway system linking the mining area of central Cornwall to the coast; the Luxulyan Valley forms a natural route for the railway to follow. To achieve this, the line had to cross the valley, and so Treffry set about solving this problem. His solution is doubly successful, as the viaduct not only carried the rails but also served as an aqueduct; it is still possible to see water running under the top layer of stones on the viaduct. The water was used to power waterwheels that enabled the railway to move loads up the steep incline. For the water to flow, the angle of the viaduct had to be accurate. The railway was completed in 1844, and began service. Treffry continued to improve his mineral links, and his railways stretched from Newquay – which became a popular resort – across Cornwall and to the local south-coast ports. Treffry died of pneumonia in 1850, but his achievements lived on and supported the work of others. Today, we are left to marvel at his vision and engineering acumen.

Truro Cathedral

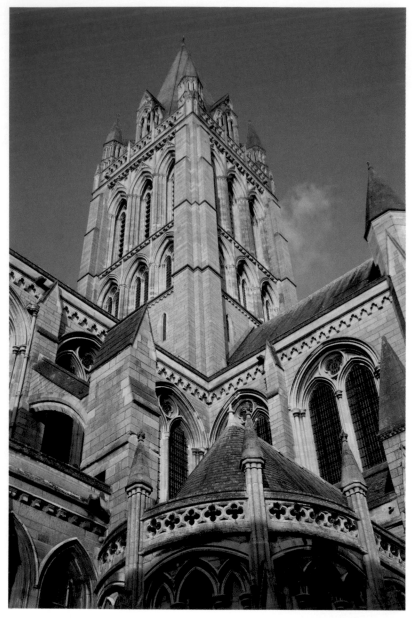

Right: Truro Cathedral by night.
Above: Truro Cathedral.

The clean lines of the cathedral towers dominate the city of Truro. This admirable building is an astonishing achievement in so many ways, not least because it is one of this country's younger cathedrals.

When it was built between 1880 and 1910 it became the first cathedral to be erected on a new site since 1220, and the first new cathedral since St Paul's in London. Before then, Truro had only minor importance in the county as a port and a stannary town. All the major administrative functions were linked to Bodmin. Money from the tin industry changed Truro; it became a focus for the important and wealthy, and in 1877 it was granted city status by Queen Victoria.

It is a surprising fact that from the tenth century until the late nineteenth century Cornwall did not have its own diocese, but was combined with Devon. When finally this was granted, the bishop was to be based in Truro, and this required a powerful, impressive new building.

The first Bishop, Bishop Benson, led fund-raising which enabled the building of a new cathedral to start in 1880; the cathedral was consecrated in 1889, and finally completed in 1910. What a remarkable testament to Victorian ambition: the building had to be squeezed into the space available between shops and houses. The architect, John Pearson, created a Gothic-style cathedral with soaring pillars and pointed arches; he was also able to incorporate part of the parish church, which can now be seen as St Mary's aisle. The central tower reaches to a height of 76 metres, and can be seen from miles around. The building materials of granite and Bath stone provide a creamy colour, so that whatever the season the interior is warm and welcoming.

The rose windows, which represent the Holy Trinity, are a wonderful example of Victorian stained glass. Standing between those of the north and south transepts, the eye is captured by glorious reds and pinks. These windows are extremely important, as examples of glass work from this time are rare, and the petal-like shapes of these rose windows are picked up throughout the architecture, giving the building a wonderful coherence.

Like any great building, this cathedral has evolved over the years. The Chapter House was added in 1967, and now houses a refectory and gift shop. Sadly the Bath stone has not faired well in the Cornish weather and restoration is necessary, but this is a building worth the effort.

In winter, the headland of West Pentire looks like many other Cornish headlands. In summer, the same headland looks like nothing else on Earth, and the transformation is down to a few weeds – arable weeds!

Visit this headland in late June or early July and it is impossible to be unmoved by the spectacle. This is when the fields come to life with the most amazing natural display of flowers imaginable. The dominant flowers in the fields here are corn marigolds and poppies. The contrast brought by their yellow and red flowers is absolutely stunning, and when you consider that the backdrop to this display is provided by the blue ocean, and occasionally a blue sky, the spectacle is complete.

This place is iconic for no other reason than its sheer, unadulterated beauty, but it is also a very valuable habitat for some quite unusual flowers. The headland protects some 154 species of arable weeds; many are extremely rare, and some do not exist in other parts of Cornwall. Most visitors will not get past identifying the corn marigolds and poppies, and though that doesn't matter it is interesting to note that there are in fact three different species of poppy in these fields.

The common poppies have large, overlapping, scarlet red petals with dark centres to their flowers. Rough poppies are so named because of their roughly textured buds, but they are smaller flowers with a more crimson colour, again with dark centres. The long-headed poppy has a long seed pod, and its flowers are orange-red in colour and lack the dark centre.

The National Trust manages the fields in a similar way to which a farmer would manage any arable field, with one fairly significant difference: they don't sow a crop! The most important process that the fields undergo is an annual ploughing, because arable weeds grow best in disturbed soil. There is little point in sowing a crop to compete with the flowers when there is no desire to harvest it, so here the arable weeds can grow unhindered.

I don't want to give the impression that this spot is not worth visiting at other times of the year – nothing could be further from the truth. In April and May the uncultivated ground plays host to a tremendous showing of cowslips, particularly on the slopes leading down to nearby Polly Joke. In later May and early June the coastal fringe comes to life with the flowers of thrift and sea campion, among other wildflowers.

Left: The view of Polly Joke from West Pentire headland.
Above: Poppies growing in the fields at West Pentire.

Wheal Coates

Right: Wheal Coates sits on the coastline of St Agnes Head.
Above: Wheal Coates engine house.

Tin mining brought prosperity to a minority of people in Cornwall. It temporarily changed the lives of the masses, not always for the better, but it changed the landscape for good. There are many places where we can reflect on the history of mining, but few that are as symbolic as the Wheal Coates mine on St Agnes Head, where the preserved ruins of a bygone age sit on top of heather-clad cliffs, looking down on a glimmering sea.

The three engine houses were used for pumping, winding and stamping, as tin was brought to the surface; miners lowered down; water removed from the shafts, and the tin finished for sale. The Towanroath shaft house here is now a listed building, and guaranteed to endure as a reminder of the intense activity in the area. The mine itself opened in 1872, and worked continuously until 1889. It reopened for a short period in the early twentieth century, closing for good in 1914. A great deal of time and money were dedicated to an industry that lasted such a short time.

Wheal Coates is just one of many mines in this area. There are others along this stretch of coast (such as Wheal Kitty), and further inland to the south of St Agnes Beacon. St Agnes grew with the mining industry; the port here expanded to allow coal to be shipped in and ore to be shipped out. St Agnes itself is where the mine captains lived, in grand houses. Settlements like those at Mount Hawke and Goonbell were established to accommodate the miners; it is still possible to see the small fields around these villages that would have been the miners' smallholdings. It seems incredible now that each morning men would walk to their mine; work long hours at the bottom of a mine shaft which might have been under the sea, and then spend their spare time toiling to grow food to sustain their family. When admiring the beauty of a location such as this, it is easy to romanticize about the miner's way of life, but the truth is that mining was only really profitable for a minority; for most it was a harsh existence, and a real risk to health.

This area is protected for a variety of purposes: the old mining buildings and other associated remains are designated as one part of the World Heritage Site. The heathland, which looks beautiful in late summer with ling, bell heather and western gorse all in flower simultaneously, is also the focus of conservation work under the auspices of the HEATH (heathland, environment, agriculture, tourism and heritage) project.

Notes on the Locations

Abbey Garden, Tresco (pages 6–7): For information about Tresco and the Abbey Garden, on the Isles of Scilly, see www.tresco.co.uk. Entrance fee.

Bedruthan Steps (pages 8–9): National Trust. Car-park at SW 852 696 off the B3276 north of Mawgan Porth. Access all year, toilets and shop in car-park. Access to beach only possible in summer; check tides carefully.

Boscastle Harbour (pages 10–11): Car-park and visitor centre (tel. 01840 250010) for Boscastle at SX 100 914 on the B3263. Beeny Cliff is approximately 3.2 km along the coast to the north of Boscastle harbour. Forrabury Common is to the south of the harbour. St Juliot's church is at SX 128 913.

Botallack (pages 12–13): Turn off the B3306 at Botallack, and follow the track seawards, parking around the old Count House (National Trust). The Count House has information about the area, and toilets. The Crowns engine houses are at SW 363 336.

Caerhays Castle (pages 14–15): Gorran, St Austell (tel. 01872 501310 or 501144, www.caerhays.co.uk). SW 972 417. Garden and house opening times vary each year, but are around February/March until June; it is advisable to check. Entrance fee.

Carn Brea (pages 16–17): Monument is at SW 684 407. Follow the road/track from Carnkie (SW 686 399). Parking near the top of the hill.

Carn Euny (pages 18–19): English Heritage. The site is signposted from the A30 at Drift, south-west of Penzance. SW 402 288. For Halliggye fogou follow signs to Trelowarren from the B3293, south of Helston, fogou at SW 714 239. Chysauster SW474 350, also English Heritage.

Castle-an-Dinas (pages 20–21): Access from the A39 close to St Columb; head towards Tregonetha on the minor road, signposted left from here. Parking at SW 944 620; hill fort at SW 945 624. Bosigran cliff castle is at SW 416 371; parking and access from the B3306 at Rosemergy, west of Zennor.

Charlestown Harbour (pages 22–23): Follow signs from the A390 in St Austell, parking at SW 517 038. The main harbour area is pedestrian only. Charlestown Shipwreck and Heritage Centre (tel. 01726 69897, www.shipwreckcharlestown.com). Entrance fee.

China Clay Tips (pages 24–25): For information and history of china clay mining visit the China Clay Country Park, Wheal Martyn, Carthew, St Austell (tel. 01726 850362, www.wheal-martyn.com). Entrance fee. Caerloggas Downs, near Stenalees, north of St Austell, viewpoint at SX 019 565.

Come-to-Good (pages 26–27): Meeting House at SW 814 404, follow signs from Carnon Downs on the A39. Meetings take place at 10.30 a.m. each Sunday.

Cot Valley (pages 28–29): In St Just take the road towards Cape Cornwall, then turn left by the primary school. This is a narrow road with parking at the very end near the beach. SW 355 308.

The Eden Project (pages 30–31): Near St Austell, well signposted from major routes, including A30. SX 048 547 (tel. 01726 811911, www.edenproject.com). Entrance fee.

Fistral Beach (pages 32–33): The beach is west of Newquay; car-park at SW 802 623. Cribbar Rocks SW 797 630.

Fowey (pages 34–35): Fowey Tourist Information Centre (tel. 01726 833616). For festival information and bookings see www.dumaurierfestival.co.uk.

Gig Racing (pages 36–37): World pilot gig championships see www.worldgigs.co.uk. Nut Rock SV 891 126; St Mary's harbour SV 904 110. Information from Isles of Scilly Tourist Information Centre (tel. 01720 422536).

Godrevy (pages 38–39): Car-parking owned by National Trust, signposted from the B3011 north of Hayle. For the lighthouse park at the end of the track, SW 582 432; Mutton Cove SW 584 434.

Goonhilly Earth Station (pages 40–41): Goonhilly Satellite Earth Station visitor centre on B3293 from Helston towards St Keverne (tel. 0800 679 593, www.goonhilly.bt.com). SW 727 214. Entrance fee.

Gunwalloe Church Cove (pages 42–43): Gunwalloe Church Cove car-park (National Trust) at SW 659 208. The church is at SW 661 206. Follow signs from the A3083 near Culdrose, south of Helston.

Gwennap Pit (pages 44–45): Signposted from the B3298 at the south end of Carharrack, visitor centre at SW 716 417, limited parking.

Hell Bay (pages 46–47): Bryher, Isles of Scilly, SV 876 159.

Helston Flora (pages 48–49): Helston Tourist Information Centre (tel. 01326 565431, www.helstonfloraday.org.uk).

Holy Wells (pages 50–51): St Keyne's Well is just off the B3254 at SX 248 603 north of Looe. Madron Well on the Madron to Morvah road, north-west of Penzance, is at SW 446 328.

Jamaica Inn (pages 52–53): The inn is just off the A30 at Bolventor at SX 183 767, (tel. 01566 86250, www.jamaicainn. co.uk).

King Harry Ferry (pages 54–55): For timetable information see www.kingharry-info.co.uk. The ferry is on the B3289, Trelissick side at SW 841 396. Be prepared to queue at peak times.

Kit Hill (pages 56–57): From the A390 near Callington take the B3257 and follow signs to the hill. Car-parks at three locations, all on the east side of the hill; the highest at SX 375 714, close to the summit.

Kynance Cove (pages 58–59): Kynance Cove is owned by the National Trust, car-parking at SW 687 134, signposted from the A3083 near Lizard village.

Land's End (pages 60–61): Follow the A30 to its end, park in the theme park car-park, SW 345 250. The coastal footpath is accessed from the car-park. For more information about the theme park, tickets and opening times see www.landsend-landmark.co.uk.

Lanhydrock (pages 62–63): National Trust. Signposted from the A38 and A30 near Bodmin; car-parking at SX 087 643 (tel. 01208 265950). Entrance fee for non-members.

Lanyon Quoit (pages 64–65): Access from the Madron to Morvah road, north-west of Penzance. The quoit is close to the road, and easily reached at SW 430 336. Chûn Quoit and Chûn Castle SW405339; access from the B3318 near Pendeen.

Launceston Castle (pages 66–67): English Heritage (tel. 01566 772365). Easily located in Launceston at SX 330 846. Entrance fee for non-members.

Lizard Point (pages 68–69): Parking in Lizard village or at SW 703 116. Footpaths to the point and around the coast easily accessed from the car-park.

Men-an-Tol (pages 70–71): Access from the Madron to Morvah road. Near to Morvah, find a small lay-by near Bosullow at SW 418 344; follow the footpath to the north-east. Men-an-Tol is at SW 427 349.

Morwenstow (pages 72–73): To reach the village follow signs from A39 near Kilkhampton, parking at SS 207 154 close to the church. Footpaths from village lead to the cliffs and Hawker's Hut, SS 199 153. National Trust, but open to all.

Mousehole (pages 74–75): Village signposted from the B3315; car-park SW 473 266, harbour SW 470 263. See www. mouseholelights.com for dates of the Christmas lights.

National Maritime Museum (pages 76–77): The museum is close to Falmouth Docks at SW 815 324. For information about opening and exhibitions tel. 01326 313388, or see www.nmmc.co.uk. Entrance fee.

Newlyn Harbour (pages 78–79): Signposted from A30 past Penzance. Harbour around SW 465 287. Penlee House Gallery and Museum is in Penzance (tel. 01736 363625, www.penleehouse.org.uk).

Padstow (pages 80–81): Padstow is reached from the A389 west of Wadebridge. There are several car-parks in the town. The Camel Trail starts at SW 922 751, or Wadebridge SW 989 726. There are cycle hire shops at each end.

Polperro (pages 82–83): Follow the A387 from Looe, parking at SX 206 516. Limited car access into village. Harbour at SX 209 509.

Poltesco (pages 84–85): North-east of Cadgwith, SW 727 157. Limited parking at Poltesco; access on foot from Cadgwith.

Port Isaac (pages 86–87): Follow the B3267, car-parking at SW 999 810; harbour at SW 996 808. Port Quinn SW 972 806.

Porthcurno (pages 88–89): Minack Theatre at SW 387 221, follow signs from the A30 west of Penzance. Information and box office tel. 01736 810181, or see www.minack.com. Entrance fee. Porthcurno Telegraph Museum SW 385 227, also signposted from the A30 (tel. 01736 810966, www.porth-curno.org.uk). Entrance fee. Logan Rock is at SW 398 219.

Restormel Castle (pages 90–91): English Heritage. Follow signs from the A390 in Lostwithiel, castle at SX 104 614. Entrance fee for non-members.

Roche Rock (pages 92–93): Just outside Roche off the B3274 at SW 992 596. Free access.

Smuggler's Cottage (pages 94–95): Follow signs from the B3289, on the Roseland side of the King Harry Ferry, SW 844 403. To contact the inn tel. 01872 580309, or see www.tolverneriverfal.co.uk.

St Enodoc (pages 96–97): Rock lifeboat station at SW 929 756. For information about the RNLI see www.rnli.org.uk. St Enodoc Church SW 932 773, park at Trebetherick Beach car-park or in Rock.

St George's Island (Looe Island) (pages 98–99): Boat trips from Looe, depending on tides. For more information about the island contact Cornwall Wildlife Trust, tel. 01872 273939, or see www.cornwallwildlifetrust.org.uk. *We Bought an Island* (1976) and *Tales from our Cornish Island* (1986) by Evelyn Atkins, published by Harrap, London, and Alexander Associates, Fowey.

St Mawes & Pendennis Castles (pages 100–101): English Heritage. St Mawes Castle at SW 842 328, Pendennis Castle, Falmouth at SW 826 318. Entrance fee for non-members.

St Michael's Mount (pages 102–103): Castle on the Mount is owned by the National Trust. Entrance fee for non-members. Access to the Mount is free if you walk across the causeway from Marazion; boat service at high tide. Castle at SW 515 298.

St Piran's Chapel (pages 104–105): Site of St Piran's Oratory SW 767564; St Piran's church SW 772 566, park on minor road north-east of Perranporth at SW 775 554. The St Piran's Day march starts from Perran Sands Holiday Centre (SW 765 557). For information about St Piran's Day events see www.an-daras.com.

Stone Circles (pages 106–107): Merry Maidens near Lamorna SW 434 245; The Hurlers, close to Minions SX 258 714; Duloe stone circle SX 236 583, access from the B3254 in Duloe.

Tamar Bridges (pages 108–109): There is a viewing point for the bridges at SX 439 587 just off the A38 on the Plymouth side of the bridges, or view from Saltash. The road bridge has foot access.

Tate St Ives (pages 110–111): Tate St Ives is at Porthmeor Beach, SW 516 408; Barbara Hepworth Museum and Sculpture Garden at Barnoon Hill SW 517 406. Information about both from the Tate Gallery (tel. 01736 796226, www.tate.org.uk/stives). Entrance fee.

Tintagel (pages 112–113): English Heritage. Access from coastal footpath at SX 051 890, approx. 0.5 km from the centre of Tintagel. Entrance fee for non-members.

Tors of Bodmin Moor (pages 114–115): Brown Willy summit at SX 158 800. Roughtor at SX 146 807, parking for the tor at SX 138 818. To reach this road turn off the A39 in Camelford. Cheesewring at SX 257 724, park at Minions, near Upton Cross.

Trebah Garden (pages 116–117): Trebah Garden, Mawnan Smith, south of Falmouth SW 768 275 (tel. 01326 252200, www.trebah-garden.co.uk). Entrance fee.

Treffry Viaduct (pages 118–119): The viaduct is at SX 056 572 close to Luxulyan; parking at SX 058 573.

Truro Cathedral (pages 120–121): Cathedral in central Truro at SW 823 449. For information about the building and services see www.trurocathedral.org.uk.

West Pentire (pages 122–123): National Trust. Follow signs from the A3075 to the south of Newquay, drive through the village of Crantock to the end of the road. Walk from SW 776 606, car-parking at this point.

Wheal Coates (pages 124–125): National Trust. Close to St Agnes, parking at SW 703 500. Mine buildings at SW 699 501.